Inline

CONTENTS

The timing given for recipes are for a 650 watt (I.E.C. 705) oven followed in brackets by timings for a 750-800 watt (I.E.C. 705) oven, unless otherwise stated.

Published by Inline Print Limited Units 25-26 Aberdare Enterprise Centre, Aberdare, Mid Glamorgan, South Wales.

ISBN 1 872182 00 3

Recipes developed by Jean Powell in the Hitachi Test Kitchen.

Designed and Printed by Inline Print Ltd.

Photography by Harry Williams.

Illustrations by Dave Evans.

Set in Scantext Gentleman by Afal Typesetters Cardiff.

Cookware for photography kindly supplied by David Morgan Ltd of Cardiff.

INTRODUCTION

Welcome to microwave cooking! Your new microwave will help you cook meals quickly and efficiently. The microwave has many advantages of convenience over other kinds of cooking and many dishes actually give better results when cooked in a microwave oven. Here are some of the ways in which the microwave oven compliments the conventional cooker.

* You can cook quickly and economically. Unlike a conventional oven, a microwave oven does not need to be preheated and there is no wasted space when you cook small quantities.
* A microwave oven is quick and convenient for the preparation of dishes which can then be cooked by either microwave or conventional means.
* The microwave oven is the quickest and safest method for defrosting frozen foods.

Foods which cook particularly well in the microwave oven include chicken and fish, vegetables, fruit, egg dishes and puddings; the results are often superior to those produced by conventional cooking methods. Many other foods can be cooked in a microwave oven; you should experiment, test and decide what suits your particular taste.

Not all foods and cooking methods are suitable for microwave cooking. The following should not be attempted in a standard microwave oven: Yorkshire Puddings and batters, flaky, rough puff and choux pastry, eggs in their shells and deep and shallow fat frying.

How Microwaves Cook Food

Microwaves are absorbed by the water which is present in all foods. They cause such rapid friction of the water molecules that sufficient heat is created to cook foodstuffs. Microwaves penetrate to a depth of 3 to 5 cm/1½ to 2 inches; food cooks through to the middle by conduction of heat from the outer edges towards the centre.

Microwaves draw water to the surface of the food during cooking; the water subsequently evaporates, thus preventing cakes, pastry and bread from browning or forming a crust.

Fats are drawn to the surface of larger cuts of meat, causing them to caramelise and brown as they would if cooked conventionally. However the short cooking time needed for small cuts or portions is not sufficient to allow them to brown. Meats containing bones will cook fairly quickly since the bones conduct heat; however, boneless meat cooks more evenly.

Generally, foods with a high sugar or fat content cook more quickly; for instance, a syrup-coated sponge pudding will cook in two-thirds the time needed for a plain sponge pudding.

Microwave Cooking Techniques

Microwave cooking, like all techniques, needs to be learned and practised. Do not approach your new microwave oven for the first time ready to cook the Sunday lunch! Select one dish from your menu and cook it in the microwave oven; cook the rest by conventional means. When you are familiar with the techniques of microwave cookery, you can progress to using your microwave oven for the maximum range of dishes. (see First Steps p.11).

In a microwave oven, the cooking process cannot begin unless the door is closed properly. All Hitachi microwave ovens feature a built-in door seal which ensures complete safety when operating the oven.

Cooking times vary according to the weight and density of the food being cooked; the smaller the quantity and lower the density, the shorter the cooking time. As a rough guide, food needs about 75% less cooking time than in a conventional oven. To obtain best results, food should be of even size and shape. The food also needs to be arranged inside the oven so as to cook evenly. Chicken portions, chops, jacket potatoes and other bulky foods should be arranged in a circle, with the denser parts towards the outside of the turntable or plate. Complete meals on plates should be arranged so that the food is distributed in an even layer.

Microwave energy is reflected off the metal interior walls of the oven back into the food. This is one reason why metal utensils are not suitable for use in a microwave oven, and foil should only be used in special cases (see page 10). Metal also deflects energy away from the food, thus slowing down the cooking process. However, an even more important reason is the fact that some metal if used in a microwave oven can cause arcing (blue flashes). This is liable to damage the magnetron or

INTRODUCTION

the cavity of the oven. Some Hitachi ovens with browning facilities are supplied with metal racks that are designed especially for use with these models and instruction on how to use them appears with each operating guide.

Always check to ensure that no leaded glass, or china or glass with a metallic pattern or inscription are put into your microwave oven. Equally dangerous are metal staples or tags and laminated foil papers.

Since microwave energy is absorbed only by water molecules, the oven cavity and dishes remain relatively cool. This eliminates the danger of burning yourself on the sides of a hot oven when removing food from it. The microwaves penetrate through glass and plastic to the food, so while the food becomes very hot the dishes only get warm.

Steam builds up inside food in covered containers, so care is needed when removing lids or covering from such food.

Hitachi ovens have a turntable to ensure even cooking. It only revolves when the oven is in use and is removable for easy cleaning.

'Standing and Resting Time'

Microwave cooking uses a few words and phrases which need explanation. An important one is 'standing time' or 'resting time'. As explained earlier, microwave energy causes rapid friction of water molecules in food. The effect can be compared to that of a bag of pingpong balls being shaken vigorously. When the energy is switched off, the friction does not cease immediately but subsides gradually, thus continuing the cooking process — a sort of settling period after the shake-up. 'Standing time' or 'resting time' allows the heat from the outer edges of the food to cook the centre. So always slightly undercook the food and allow resting time to finish it off before testing. If it still seems underdone, you can return the food to the oven for a minute or two; this will not affect it adversely.

The length of standing time varies. For example, a rich fruit cake may need between 30 and 60 minutes, whereas a Victoria sponge may only require 5 to 10 minutes. It all depends on the volume and density of the food. Generally, the longer the cooking time, the longer the standing time.

So, remember the Microwave Cooking Code:—

If food is not cooked or PIPING HOT RIGHT THROUGH, even after following recommended cooking times, then cook it until it is, just as you would with conventional cooking.

REMEMBER: If you follow the Code and good hygiene practice in the kitchen, your microwave oven will cook absolutely safely.

Covering Food in the Oven

Most dishes cooked in a microwave oven should be covered with a casserole lid or a plate. This traps the steam, which helps the cooking process and keeps the food moist. When reheating meals on a plate, cover with another plate, to prevent them from drying out. When using cooking film it is not always necessary to pierce it as it becomes porous at 100°C/212°F; however if the cooking cycle is long, it would be better to pierce it once in the middle. If the film is not pierced before cooking, it will cause a vacuum when the dish is left to stand, so it should be pierced after cooking to prevent the food from being 'flattened'. Do not allow cooking film to come into contact with food with a high fat content.

Always be careful when removing the covering; steam has built up underneath, and you could be scalded by it so lift lids or film away from your face.

Sauces, beverages and soups do not need to be covered — you will need access to stir them.

Bread and pastry items should be left uncovered and placed on plain kitchen paper to absorb moisture.

Defrosting Food

Defrosting works by pulsing the microwave energy on and off, thus allowing the food to unfreeze without cooking it. The touch control ovens have 'contour defrost' which is a cycle of different power levels to defrost food evenly without the edges beginning to cook. This means that with most foods you can programme the oven to defrost followed by cook without needing to stand food in between. Large food items such as joints or poultry may need two shorter cycles of defrosting with a resting period in between. Bulky foods should be left for at least 10 minutes before cooking, to allow the temperature to equalise. Defrosting times will vary according to the food, but a guide is 8 to 10 minutes per 450 g/1 lb frozen food.

Drain away any water which collects while defrosting, as the water attracts energy away from the food and will slow the operation. Individual portions defrost more quickly than large amounts.

Defrosting Tips

* Underestimate defrosting times — defrosting will continue during the standing time on larger bulky items.
* Open cartons, remove lids from jars and container and slit plastic bags or pouches before placing them in the oven, as food expands when defrosting.
* Place frozen food in a larger container than it was frozen in. This allows for stirring the food without spillage.
* To speed up thawing, separate frozen foods such as chops into pieces as they start to thaw, and gently break down frozen casseroles and meat sauces moving frozen parts to the outside edge of the container.
* Fish, vegetables and meat can be defrosted in their packages but should have metal ties removed and vacuum packs slit.
* Place cakes, pastry and bread on kitchen paper to absorb moisture.

DEFROSTING GUIDE

Food	*Approx Time on Defrosting Setting*	*Procedure*	*Standing Time where necessary*
MEAT			
Beef			
Roasting Joints	*10 Minutes per 450g/1 lb*	*Place in a shallow dish and turn regularly during defrosting. Allow to rest if meat shows any signs of cooking.*	*15-20 Minutes*
Minced Beef	*10 Minutes per 450g/1 lb*	*Leave wrapped, turn over after 4 minutes, unwrap and break meat up. If centre is still frozen defrost centre for 1½ minutes longer.*	
Cubed Steak	*8-10 Minutes per 450g/1 lb*	*Start thawing in wrapper. Turn over and break up after 4 minutes.*	
Steak 1.5cm/ ¾in thick	*10 Minutes per 450g/1 lb*	*Begin defrosting in wrapper. After half defrosting turn and unwrap. Separate as soon as possible.*	
Hamburger	*11 Minutes per 450g/1 lb*	*Thaw in wrapper and turn over after half defrosting time. Separate as soon as possible.*	
Lamb			
Roasting Joints	*8-10 Minutes per 450g/1 lb*	*Stand in a shallow dish and shield any vulnerable areas (e.g. end of the leg) with foil. Turn over during defrosting.*	*15-20 Minutes*
Lamb Chops	*10 Minutes per 450g/1 lb*	*Thaw in wrapping. Turn over after half defrosting time. Separate as soon as possible.*	
Pork			
Roasting Joints	*9 Minutes per 450g/1 lb*	*Stand in a shallow dish and shield any vulnerable areas with foil. Turn during defrosting*	*15-20 Minutes*
Pork Chops	*8-10 Minutes per 450g/1 lb*	*Thaw in wrapping. Turn over after half defrosting time and separate as soon as possible.*	
Sausages	*6 Minutes per 450g/1 lb*	*Separate during defrosting.*	
Bacon	*3-4 Minutes per 225g/8 oz*	*Remove slices from pack and separate as soon as possible.*	
Liver	*5-6 Minutes per 450g/1 lb*	*Separate slices as soon as possible.*	
Kidney	*5-6 Minutes per 450g/1 lb*	*Separate during defrosting.*	
POULTRY			
Chicken/Turkey (whole)	*10 Minutes per 450g/1 lb*	*Start defrosting in wrapping, turn over after half defrosting time. The wings and legs may need to be covered with foil to prevent heating.*	*Chicken — 20 Minutes Turkey — 1-2 Hours*
Chicken Portions	*8-10 Minutes per 450g/1 lb*	*Separate as soon as possible*	
Chicken Breasts Boneless	*8-10 Minutes per 225g/8 oz*	*Separate as soon as possible.*	

Manual control models that defrost on one level will need slightly less time than those given above.

INTRODUCTION

Food	Approx Time on Defrosting Setting	Procedure	Standing Time where necessary
FISH			
White Fish Fillets	6 Minutes per 450g/1 lb	Separate as soon as possible.	
White Fish Steaks	8 Minutes per 450g/1 lb	Turn over half way through defrosting.	
Oily Fish (whole)	8 Minutes per 450g/1 lb	Turn over half way through defrosting.	
Kipper Fillets	3-4 Minutes per 225g/8 oz		
Prawns/Shrimps	4 Minutes per 225g/8 oz	Break up after 2 minutes.	
FRUIT			
Soft Fruit eg Raspberries	8-10 Minutes per 450g/1 lb	Stir gently during defrosting.	
Fruit Purées	5 Minutes 150 ml/¼ pint	Stir during defrosting.	
BREAD			
Large Loaf	8-10 Minutes	Stand on paper towel and turn once during defrosting.	
Small Loaf	5-7 Minutes	Stand on paper towel.	
Bread Rolls × 2 Crumpets × 2	20-30 Seconds	Place on paper towel.	
Pitta Bread × 2	40-70 Seconds	Place on paper towel.	
CAKES			
Sponge Cake	2 Minutes per 450g/1 lb	Place on paper towel.	
Small Cakes/ Buns ×4	2 Minutes	Place on paper towel.	
Fruit Cake	5-7 Minutes per 675g/1½ lb	Place on paper towel.	
PASTRY			
Short Crust and Puff	1¼ Minutes per 225g/8 oz		10 Minutes
Fruit Pie	5-10 Minutes per 575g/1¼ lb	Transfer from foil pie dish to glass pie dish	5 Minutes
DESSERTS			
Individual Mousse	40 Seconds		2-3 Minutes
Individual Trifle	60-70 Seconds		2-3 Minutes

Manual control models that defrost on one level will need slightly less time than those given above.

INTRODUCTION

Reheating Food

Most foods need to be covered to hold in heat and moisture during reheating; the exception is food which requires stirring, such as soups and beverages or pastry products.

The temperature of the food will affect your timings, food from the refrigerator will take longer than food stored at room temperature. It must also be remembered that standing time is required after reheating and before serving. If your oven has a metal turntable place food on the low rack provided for more efficient reheating.

Plated meals should be reheated with the thinner pieces of food in the middle and denser pieces around the outside. For plated meals with which you are serving gravy, heat the gravy separately in a small container and pour it over the reheated meal. This will ensure much more even reheating and a better end result.

Make sure food is hot and not just warm to ensure that any harmful bacteria that may be present are destroyed. Liquids should be stirred during heating and should bubble (ie. come to the boil). Where possible re-arrange food during cooking for even reheating.

Foods such as lasagne, pies, plated meals, that cannot be stirred should be heated until the centre is hot — test the centre of the base of the container or plate. If using a thermometer to check the temperature of food it should read at least 75°C (170°F) in all parts of the food.

Do not overheat pastry products — remember the filling contains more water than the pastry and will become hot quickly whilst the pastry may still feel cool. Overheating causes the filling to create steam under the pastry which then becomes soggy. For good results heat pastry products on a rack or a piece of kitchen paper and allow to stand a minute or two after cooking.

Your oven is rated to a new standard I.E.C. 705 (Part II). This new rating is in line with the Ministry of Agriculture, Fisheries and Food's request to standardise power ratings to enable food suppliers to give more accurate cooking instructions on their packaging. In order to make this easier for you to understand, ovens will be rated with a symbol that food manufacturers will use with appropriate timings. When following instructions on food packaging, use the symbol timings where given appropriate to your oven, if not, refer to the reheating chart on Page 8 of this book.

With 750-800 watt ovens some foods are better reheated using a lower power level and increasing the time. A guide is listed below.

Power level	Type of food
High	Foods which contain liquid that can be stirred (soups, drinks, meat sauces).
Medium high — increase the time for high power by ⅓rd, (e.g. 3 minutes will become 4 minutes).	Food that requires a more gentle heat e.g. vegetables, plated meals, fish dishes.
Medium — double the time for high power.	Dense foods such as cottage pie, lasagne and foods which cannot be stirred. Reheating will be slower than when using high power but it will be a better result as outer edges will not be overcooked in attempting to heat through to the centre. Meat or poultry casseroles where slower reheating will improve texture and flavour.

Heating of Baby Milk and Food

It is *NOT* recommended to sterilise babies' bottles in the microwave. Boiling water in bottles can cause pressure to build up inside the bottle and cause an explosion.

Babies' feeding bottles of milk can be warmed in the microwave using *MEDIUM POWER* to control the rapid rise in temperature. **Remove teats and all bottle lids before heating.** Times will vary according to the quantity of milk but a guideline is set out below. The bottle should then be well shaken and the temperature tested *BEFORE* feeding to the baby. If mixing baby milk powder with cold boiled water in the feeding bottle, care must be taken to ensure that the powder is thoroughly dissolved. Undissolved powder floating on the surface can become combustible when reheated in a microwave.

Likewise ready prepared baby foods can be heated in the microwave, again using *MEDIUM POWER*. For a jar of baby food, remove the lid and heat according to the chart below, stir well and test the temperature *BEFORE* feeding. Tinned foods need transferring to a suitable container *BEFORE* heating.

Heating Bottled Baby Milk

140 ml/4 oz feed — MEDIUM POWER — 30(20) seconds
250 ml/8 oz feed — MEDIUM POWER — 60(40) seconds

Shake well and test before feeding.

These timings are given for milk stored in a refrigerator. Less time is required if milk is already at room temperature.

Remember the milk only needs to be at blood heat and not as warm as we expect drinks to be.

Timings given are for 650 [750-800] watt (I.E.C. 705) ovens.

Baby Meals in Jar

110 g/4 oz 1st Stage Food — MEDIUM POWER — 40(30) seconds
150 g/5 oz 2nd Stage Food — MEDIUM POWER — 40(30) seconds

Timings are for food at normal storage temperatures.

Remember to remove lids from jars or transfer tinned food to a suitable dish *BEFORE* heating. Stir well and test *BEFORE* feeding.

INTRODUCTION

REHEATING PREPARED CONVENIENCE FOODS

Food	*Time on High*	*Special Notes*
Individual Meat Pie *Large Family Meat Pie*	*2 [1½] Minutes* *5 [4½] Minutes*	*Place on kitchen paper or rack. Stand 2-4 minutes*
Cornish Pasty *Individual Savoury Flan* *Large Family Savoury Flan*	*90 [80] Seconds* *60-90 [40-60] Seconds* *3½ [2½] Minutes*	*As above* *As above. Stand 1 minute* *As above*
Sausage Rolls × 1 *Sausage Rolls × 4* *Sausage Rolls × 12*	*20 [10] Seconds* *40-60 [30-40] Seconds* *60-90 [40-60] Seconds*	*As above* *As above. Stand 1 minute* *As above*
Pizza — Large *Pizza — Small*	*4 [2¾] Minutes* *3 [1½-2] Minutes*	*Place on rack or kitchen paper. Stand 2 minutes*
Mince Pies × 1 *Mince Pies × 4* *Mince Pies × 12*	*10 [10] Seconds* *40-60 [30-40] Seconds* *60-90 [40-60] Seconds*	*Place on rack or kitchen paper. Stand 1 minute*
Ready Cooked Sausages × 2 *Ready Cooked Sausages × 4* *Hotdog (1 Cooked Sausage in Bread Roll)*	*30-40 [20-30] Seconds* *60 [40] Seconds* *20-30 [10-20] Seconds*	*Wrap in kitchen paper. Stand 1 minute*
Plated Meal	*3-4 [2½] Minutes*	*Cover with lid or plate. Stand 1-2 minutes*
Canned Spaghetti/ Baked Beans	*1½ [1¼] Minutes per 225g/8 oz* *3 [2] Minutes per 425g/15 oz*	*Turn into bowl — stir halfway — cover to prevent splattering*
Canned Soup	*2-3 [1½-2] Minutes per 300 ml/½ pint* *4-5 [3-4] Minutes per 600 ml/1 pint*	*Turn into bowl — stir halfway through cooking to distribute heat*
Canned Steak and Kidney	*4-5 [3-4] Minutes per 440g/15½ oz*	*As above*
Canned Rice Pudding	*3 [2] Minutes per 425g/15 oz*	*Turn into bowl before heating — stir halfway through*
Canned Sponge Pudding	*2 [1½] Minutes per 275g/10 oz*	*Turn onto plate cover and reheat. Stand 1 minute*
Christmas Pudding	*2½ [2] Minutes per 450g/1 lb* *30-60 [30-40] Seconds per 1 portion*	*Stand for 2 Minutes* *Stand for 1 Minute*
Canned Vegetables	*2-3 [1½-2] Minutes per 225g/8 oz*	*Remove from can before heating*
Melting Chocolate	*60-90 [40-60] Seconds per 100g/4 oz*	*Stir well after melting*
Dissolving Jelly	*60 [50] Seconds per 135g/5 oz*	*Place in a measuring jug — stir well and add liquid up to 600 ml/1 pint*
Dissolving Gelatine	*40 [30] Seconds per 15g/½ oz*	*Sprinkle gelatine onto 3 tablespoons water before heating — stir well to dissolve*

The above timings are guidelines for reheating some popular convenience foods. However these times can vary, depending upon the temperature food has been stored at, the dishes used to reheat in and the size of individual food items such as, sausage rolls. It is important that ready prepared chilled foods are stored at correct refrigeration temperatures and are then reheated until they are piping hot and allowed to stand for the heat to equalise. If food, when tested, is not hot enough return to the oven and cook for longer. This will ensure safe reheating of foods.

DEFROSTING AND REHEATING CHART

Food	Defrost Time	Method and Standing Time	Cooking Time on High	Special Notes
Meat Casserole	*13 Minutes per 450g/1 lb* *8 Minutes per 225g/8 oz*	*Break up during defrosting*	*4-5 [3] Minutes* *2-3 [1½-2] Minutes*	*Stir before and after cooking — stand 5 minutes*
Lasagne/Moussaka	*13-15 Minutes per 450g/1 lb*	*Shield corners with foil if large dish*	*8 [6] Minutes*	*Stand 3-5 minutes*
Chilli Con Carne/ Minced Beef	*10-12 Minutes per 450g/1 lb*	*Stir halfway to break up*	*6 [5] Minutes*	*Stir half through cooking — stand 3 minutes*
Cottage Pie	*12-13 Minutes per 450g/1 lb*		*6 [5] Minutes*	*Stand 3 minutes before serving*
Boil in the Bag Entrées	*6 Minutes*	*Turn bag over during defrosting. Slit bag after defrosting*	*2 [1½] Minutes*	*Can be turned into a dish for reheating*
Pies Sweet/Savoury — Family Size	*15-20 Minutes*	*5 Minutes*	*3 [2] Minutes*	
Plated Meal	*4 Minutes*		*3-4 [2½] Minutes*	*Cover with cooking film or plate for reheating*
Pizza — Large	*Can be cooked from frozen — Place on rack or kitchen paper 300/10 oz*		*5-6 Minutes*	*Remove from any foil or base before cooking*
Sausage Rolls × 4	*1½-2 Minutes*	*Stand for 2 minutes — place on kitchen paper*	*1-2 Minutes [50-80] Seconds*	*Stand 2 minutes before serving*
Kipper Fillets boil-in-bag	*Can be cooked from frozen — Slit bag with knife 225g/8 oz*		*5-6 [3½-4] Minutes*	
Cooked Pasta	*3-4 Minutes 225g/8 oz*	*Separate with fork during defrost. Dot with butter to cook. Stand 2 Minutes.*	*3 [2] Minutes*	*Stir halfway through reheating*
Cooked Rice	*2-3 Minutes 225g/8 oz*	*Separate with fork — stand 2 Minutes*	*2 [1½] Minutes*	*Stir halfway through reheating*

Timing and Variable Power Settings

All Hitachi ovens have a timer, which gives an audible signal at the end of the cooking cycle, at which time the microwave power is automatically shut off. So provided the time has been set correctly, there is no risk of overcooking foods. Remember that timings given for microwave cooking are a guideline and may need adjusting according to the different types of dishes and quantity of food used.

Hitachi ovens have variable power settings. These can be compared to the thermostat on a conventional oven. Some foods cooked conventionally, such as stews and puddings, are best cooked on a low heat; the same applies to microwave cookery. Whilst most foods can be cooked on high power, Hitachi gives you the flexibility of being able to cook food at the most suitable power level. The oven will still appear to be working, when, in fact, the energy is pulsing on and off according to the power level chosen. These variable power settings include a defrost level, which enable you to defrost foods, quickly and safely. The medium low setting is the lowest cooking level for non-frozen foods. The low setting on Hitachi microwave ovens is a facility to keep food warm or to soften butter and margarine.

Cookware and Utensils

Some cookware and utensils you already own are suitable for use in the microwave oven. You will find ovenproof glassware ideal for microwave use. China and glazed earthenware are suitable, provided they have no gold or silver decorations or inscriptions. Unglazed earthenware is unsuitable as it is porous and will absorb the microwaves. To test the suitability of a container place it in the microwave oven and put a cup containing 250 ml/8 fl oz water on top of, or next to, the container you are testing (depending on its shape). Heat on high for 1 minute; the water should be warm and the container cool. If the container is warm it is unsuitable for use in a microwave oven.

The shape of the container is also important; round shapes and ring moulds cook more evenly than square shapes. It is also important to choose containers that are deep enough to allow liquids to boil without spilling over. Do not use narrow neck containers.

Plain kitchen paper is very useful for absorbing moisture or excess fat during cooking. It can also be used as a loose covering, to prevent food splattering the oven. Be careful using re-cycled kitchen paper as it may contain metal particles that could cause arcing or become flamable.

Wooden or plastic spoons or spatulas can be left in sauces in the microwave oven for a short time to use for stirring, but metal utensils must always be removed before the power is switched on. Wooden bowls or baskets can be used for quick reheating of bread rolls, but prolonged cooking will dry out the wood and cause cracking.

Most plastics are suitable for use in the microwave oven, though thin containers such as cream and yogurt cartons, will buckle as the food becomes hot. Foods with a high fat or sugar content may be unsuitable for microwaving in plastic containers; check the cookware manufacturer's instructions before using. Roasting bags for joints of meat or poultry, and polythene bags for cooking or blanching vegetables are also suitable, but replace the metal ties with elastic bands or plastic seals such as those used on sliced bread wrappers. Cooking film is useful for covering lidless containers, but does not always cling to plastic.

For those ovens without a browning facility some foods may need to be browned using a browning dish. The browning dish has special filaments in the base that absorb energy; it must be preheated empty (according to manufacturer's instructions). Without removing the dish from the oven the food is seared onto the hot surface. This must be done quickly as the dish does not retain heat once food is in it.

Food is then microwaved in the usual way. Use oven gloves as the dish becomes very hot.

Perhaps one of the most useful cooking utensils made especially for microwave cooking is a plastic rack for roasting meat and poultry and 'grilling' bacon. An upturned cereal bowl on a glass baking dish could substitute for a microwave-proof meat rack, as this arrangement would allow the juices and fat to drain away. The plastic rack is also useful for warming breads and pizzas, as air is allowed to circulate around the dough, preventing the base from becoming soggy.

Although most metal cannot be used in a microwave oven, aluminium foil has limited use. As explained earlier, foil reflects microwave energy away from the food. However, for this reason,

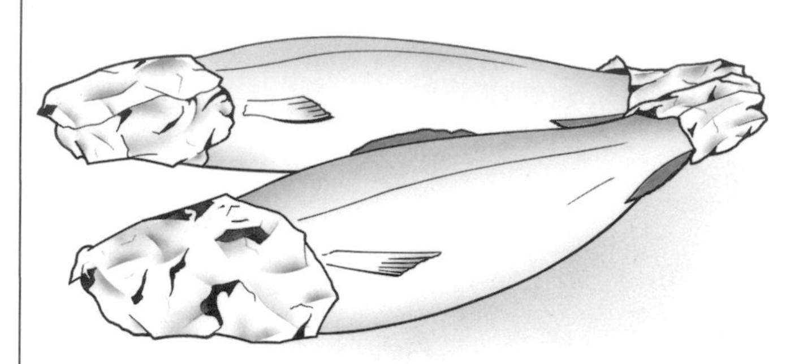

foil can be very useful in shielding sensitive areas of food from overcooking. Single pieces of foil can be wrapped around chicken wingtips or legs, or the head and tail of a fish. In this way, these areas are protected from excess microwave energy, but they will still cook by conduction of heat from the exposed surfaces. A narrow strip of foil can be placed around a fruit cake to slow down the cooking of the outer area and ensure even cooking. At no time should foil touch the walls of the oven or two or more pieces of foil be joined as this will cause arcing.

Cleaning the Oven

The oven should be kept as clean as possible, as food splashes on the walls eventually lower the efficiency of the microwaves reflected on the food.

However, another of the oven's great advantages is ease of cleaning. A microwave oven simply needs a wipe out with a warm, damp cloth after use. If food becomes dried on, simply stand a cup of water in the oven and microwave on high until it boils. Leave it in the oven for fifteen minutes; the steam from the water will soften the food particles which can then easily be wiped away.

Ovens with special browning facilities may need the occasional wipe with a non-scour cleaner to keep the oven clean.

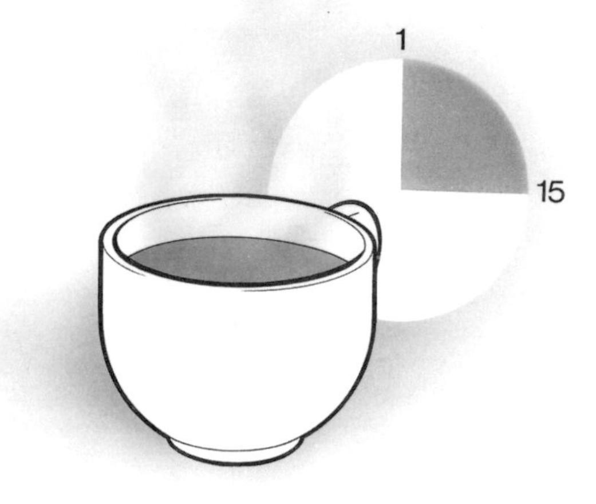

INTRODUCTION

Autosensor

Ovens with the Autosensor facility are designed to take the ease of microwave cooking one step further. No power level or time is necessary; the Autosensor cooks a whole range of foods automatically.

Food cooked using the Autosensor should be covered with a lid, plate or cooking film. While the food is cooking there is a gradual built up of steam. The steam eventually escapes in bursts from around the edges of the lidded container. This puff of steam is crucial for the Autosensor to produce accurate results. The cooker door should not be opened during the first part of the cooking cycle or it will alter this gradual build-up of steam. 'Standing time' is still very important — do not uncover until after 'standing'. (Please refer to the additional booklet that accompanies these ovens).

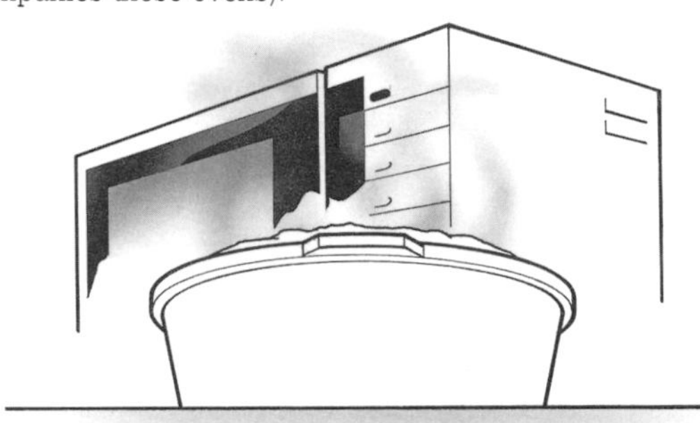

Touch Controls

Electronically advanced yet simple to operate, the touch controls enable you to programme your microwave oven for a range of operations. For example, a dish can be programmed to cook on high followed by a second cooking period at a lower power, or a dish can be reheated, then kept hot at a low setting until it is to be served.

With touch control ovens you can delay the start of cooking — very useful if you wish to have a dish ready cooked when you return home.

Memory Banks

Some models have 'memory' banks to enable regularly used recipes to be stored and recalled at the touch of a pad. Alternatively they can be used to store frequently used times, eg 3 minutes (a useful reheating time).

Weight Defrost/Weight Cook

Models with these features enable you to defrost food by programming the food type and the weight into the oven. It then calculates the time needed and automatically switches off when defrosting is complete.

Likewise, weight cook operates in the same way, programme in the food type and the weight and the oven automatically switches off when cooking is complete. The cooking time and power levels are worked out for you.

Browning Facilities

Foods cooked in the microwave, although full of flavour can sometimes lack colour due to the absense of external heat to brown and crispen the surface. Some Hitachi models have a built-in grill facility to give food a traditional look.

The Hitachi 4-way combination microwave offers the best of both worlds, the speed of microwaves combined with the traditional fan convection heat for food cooked and browned to perfection. These ovens usually have a metal turntable and it is recommended that food is placed on the low rack provided with the oven, for more efficient microwave cooking.

First Steps

It is probable that your first steps using your new microwave will be either reheating or defrosting food and making simple snacks.

Start building up your microwave experience by reheating soups and ready prepared food, cooking vegetables, chicken and fish portions, so that you can begin to understand how quickly foods cook by microwave. It is a very much faster method of cooking than any you will have been used to and it is therefore very easy to over cook food. The golden rule is to undercook, in the beginning, allow food to stand, test, then if it needs more cooking give it extra time — it will not spoil by this method but food overcooked cannot be made good.

When you are new to microwave cooking it is not a good idea to attempt to cook a whole meal by microwave. So much time will be spent consulting your cookbook and charts for each food that you will feel that you could have cooked it as quickly by the conventional means you are used to. Begin by cooking one part of the meal in the microwave and cook the remainder by conventional means. Then as your confidence grows progress to cooking other parts of the meal until you feel able to progress to meal planning.

Some of the recipes in this book are marked 'Easy' so begin with these and progress to those needing more skill as you feel your confidence grow.

Meal Planning

Most dishes are cooked individually in the microwave. Some requiring similar cooking times and power levels can be cooked together though generally speaking there is no great advantage as timings have to be increased with a larger quantity of food. How then can you cook a complete meal in the microwave and serve it hot?

Meat and poultry dishes usually require 10-20 minutes standing time and hold their heat well so begin cooking with these and progress to the vegetables. A general rule of thumb is to start with the root or 'below ground' vegetables as they require the most cooking time. Next cook 'above ground' vegetables such as greens, etc, and finally, frozen vegetables.

Fish does not hold its heat as well as meat and is often better cooked after the vegetables. When cooking is complete you may wish to reheat the first dish for a minute or two to bring it back to heat, then you are ready to serve.

Overleaf are some examples of how to plan and cook meals.

INTRODUCTION

Breakfast for Two

Porridge, *3-5 [2-3½] minutes*
Bacon, tomato and scrambled eggs *5 [3½] minutes*

1 Mix 1 cup porridge oats with ½ teaspoon salt and 2½ cups water in a bowl. Cook on medium high power for 5 [3½] minutes or high for 3-4 [2½] minutes, stir during cooking, cover and stand for 2 minutes while preparing egg and bacon.
2 Beat 2 eggs, seasoning and 2 tablespoons milk in a jug or bowl and stand in the centre of roasting rack. Place 2 bacon rashers either side of jug and halved tomato under the rack.

Cover bacon with strips of kitchen paper. Cook on high for 3 [2] minutes, stir eggs, replace and cook for a further 2 [1½] minutes on high. Stir eggs again and serve on a plate with bacon rashers and tomato.

Lunch for Four

Soup (of choice) *Varies between 13-25 minutes*
Spaghetti Bolognese (See page 67) *Spaghetti — 6 [4] minutes, Bolognese Sauce — 18 [12-13] minutes*

1 Prepare soup earlier in the day or approximately 35 minutes before the meal. Cover until required.
2 Cook spaghetti as on page 61 and cover while making the sauce.
3 Prepare and cook bolognese sauce and leave to stand.
4 While the sauce is standing reheat the soup. Reheat the spaghetti as necessary and serve with bolognese sauce.

Dinner for Four

Mushroom and Egg Cocottes (see page 18) *5 [4] minutes*
Loin of Lamb with Redcurrant Sauce (see page 35)
Lamb — 30 [20] minutes, Sauce — 5½-6½ [4] minutes
Scalloped Potatoes (see page 54) *24 [18] minutes.*
Green Beans *See Vegetable Chart for fresh or frozen times*
Old English Trifle (see page 82) — *11 [8½] minutes*

1 Prepare and cook trifle earlier in the day and chill.
2 Prepare mushrooms and egg cocottes up to sprinkling with paprika and leave aside ready to cook.
3 Prepare and cook redcurrant sauce, to serve with lamb. Set aside.
4 Prepare and cook lamb; meanwhile prepare the scalloped potatoes.
5 Wrap cooked lamb in foil and set aside. Cook scalloped potatoes and set aside.
6 Cook beans according to the vegetable chart and drain.
7 Cook mushroom and egg cocottes. Make toast and cut into fingers.
8 During the first course, reheat the sauce and the potatoes if necessary and serve with lamb and beans. Follow with Old English Trifle for dessert.

Seasonal Cooking

Seasonal cooking conjures up pictures of barbecues in summer, hot dogs and baked potatoes around an Autumn bonfire and that most seasonal event of the year, Christmas with all its trimmings. On these occasions the microwave can make a valuable contribution.

Cooking out of doors is a very popular and relaxed way of eating but once the aroma fills the air everyone wants to eat at once! Unfortunately some foods take longer to cook than others and the average barbecue can only take so much food; this is when the microwave can help to speed up the cooking.

Although sausages cook quickly on the barbecue they leak quite a lot of fat during cooking which causes the barbecue to spit and flare up. Prevent this by part cooking beforehand in the microwave and browning them off on a barbecue. Chicken joints

INTRODUCTION

can also be part cooked and then transferred to the barbecue to finish cooking for a lovely crispy skin and flavour. Marinades and sauces can be prepared beforehand in the microwave. Vegetables such as new potatoes can be cooked quickly by microwave while meat is being barbecued.

Baked potatoes can be started off in the microwave and then wrapped in foil and finished off around a bonfire.

The microwave is useful for warming garlic bread, baked beans, etc and especially for reheating foods when they have cooled after cooking out of doors.

The Christmas season always seems to involve a great deal of preparation for the big day. For many that means juggling to fit in the necessary time around a busy lifestyle. The microwave can help to achieve traditional food with the minimum of time and effort.

Preparation can begin in advance by drying herbs and cooking the new season's apples for mincemeat so that it can mature ready for the mince pies.

The Christmas pudding is traditionally made months ahead for flavours to develop. The difficulty lies not with the making of the puddings but having enough time to supervise the long hours of traditional steaming and regularly topping up the water level. A good pudding can be achieved by cooking in the microwave on Medium Low power which controls the cooking to allow the flavours to develop. Make at least two weeks before the day to allow them to mature, if storing longer than 8 weeks they are better frozen until required.

Stuffings and bread sauce can be made using the microwave to soften and cook vegetables such as duchess potatoes or creamed leeks for the freezer, to be defrosted and reheated at Christmas. Use the microwave to dissolve gelatine, jellies, melt chocolate, make caramel or custards, in the preparation of desserts.

Using the Microwave on Christmas Day

1 Blanch peeled potatoes ready for roasting — cook on High for 3 [2] minutes in a covered dish. Remove lid and allow potatoes to dry out for a minute or two then proceed to coat in roasting fat or oil and roast in the usual way.

2 Defrost apple sauce/bread sauce/brandy butter/ready prepared vegetables.

3 To cook vegetables, start with root vegetables which will take the longest to cook. Leave to stand whilst cooking 'above ground' vegetables, eg sprouts, cauliflower, etc, and finally any frozen vegetables as they cook the quickest, or reheat any pre-cooked vegetable dishes.

4 Make the gravy in a serving jug just before sitting down to eat. Cover with cooking film to prevent skin forming and keep warm until ready to serve.

5 Reheat pudding and allow to stand for a few minutes before serving
eg 450 g/1 lb pudding $2\frac{1}{2}$-3 [2-$2\frac{1}{2}$] minutes on high power
or 450 g/1 lb pudding 5 [$3\frac{1}{2}$] minutes on medium power.

7 Warm a tot of brandy on high for 20-30 [10-20] seconds, pour over pudding and ignite for a traditional presentation at the table.

8 Timings for warming mince pies and sausage rolls:
1 mince pie/sausage roll 10-20 [10] seconds
4 mince pies/sausage rolls 40 [30] seconds
12 mince pies/sausage rolls 60-90 [40-60] seconds

9 When red wine has not had time to 'breathe' pour into glasses and place in the microwave for one minute on low power to bring to room temperature.

10 To ripen soft cheeses, eg Brie — give short bursts of one minute on the low setting, until the cheese is the desired ripeness. To bring cheeses straight from the refrigerator back to room temperature, microwave for one minute on low power (remember to remove any foil wrappings before putting in the microwave).

SOUPS AND STARTERS

When making soups in the microwave, reduce the amount of liquid required in the recipe. This will shorten the cooking time; add boiling water to the required amount before serving. Packet soups should be mixed with water and left to soften for 20-30 minutes before cooking on high. Allow 6-8(4-5) minutes for 600-750 ml/1¼ pints or 10-12(7-8) minutes for 1 litre/1½ pints. Stand for 5 minutes before serving.
Canned soups can be reheated quickly and conveniently in individual bowls on high for 1½(1) minutes, or cook the contents of a 435 g/15 oz can in a basin for 3-4(2½) minutes on high, stirring halfway through heating. If you are using cream in soups, reheat on medium power so as not to curdle the cream.
Bone stock can be made quickly by cooking about 900 g/2 lb bones with seasoning and water, covered, on high, for 20(14) minutes. Leave to stand for 20 minutes before straining.

Mushroom Soup

Cooking time 22 [15] minutes Serves 4-6

350 g	*mushrooms*	*12 oz*
50 g	*butter*	*2 oz*
25 g	*flour*	*1 oz*
900 ml	*chicken stock or water*	*1½ pint*
	salt and freshly ground black pepper	
	chopped parsley	

Wipe or wash mushrooms and slice thinly. Heat butter in a large 3 pint bowl on high for 60 [40] seconds until melted. Add mushrooms and continue to cook on High for 3 [2] minutes. Stir in the flour.

Blend in the stock or water gradually. Heat on High for 10 [7] minutes to bring to boil, stirring twice. Cover and cook for further 8 [5] minutes on Medium High. Add salt and pepper to taste. Lift mushrooms out of liquid with slotted spoon and pass through a fine sieve or liquidise in a blender or food processor with a little of the liquid until smooth. Return to bowl and reheat. Garnish with chopped parsley.

NB:
Cream of Mushroom Soup — use only 1 pint chicken stock or water and ½ pint milk. Proceed as above.
Add a swirl of cream to soup just before serving.

Mushroom Soup with Bacon Garnish
Make soup as above. For garnish, cook 3-4 streaky rashers of smoked bacon on high for 3-4 [2-3] minutes, until crisp. Crumble or snip into small pieces and scatter over soup for serving.

Cream of Celery Soup

Cooking time 26-27 [19-20] minutes Serves 6-8

1	*head of Celery — washed and finely sliced*	*1*
1	*onion — finely sliced*	*1*
25 g	*butter*	*1 oz*
600 ml	*chicken stock*	*1 pint*
1	*bay leaf*	*1*
	Seasoning	
¼ tsp	*nutmeg*	*¼ tsp*
40 g	*butter*	*1½ oz*
40 g	*plain flour*	*1¼ oz*
600 ml	*milk*	*1 pint*
150 ml	*single cream*	*¼ pint*
	chopped chives for garnish	

Combine butter, celery and onion in a large dish, cover and cook on High for 5 [3½-4] minutes. Add hot chicken stock, bay leaf and seasoning and nutmeg. Cover and cook on High for 10 [7] minutes. Leave to stand 5 minutes while making sauce.

Melt 1½ oz butter in a separate bowl on High for 60 [40] seconds — stir in flour and cook on High for 60 [40] seconds. Blend in the milk and cook on High for 7-8 [5-5½] minutes stirring twice during cooking.

Remove bay leaf from celery soup and puree in a liquidiser or food processor. Pour this into the white sauce, stir in cream and adjust seasoning.

Reheat for 2(1½) minutes on High and serve garnished with chopped chives.

This soup has a lovely fresh taste of celery and can be sieved if you want a very smooth texture.

Microtip

To make melba toast, toast bread in the usual way, slice through the middle to produce two thin slices, place on plate untoasted side uppermost and microwave on high for 60-70 [40-60] seconds until dry and crisp. These can then be stored in an airtight container.

Timings given are for 650 [750-800] watt ovens

Easy

Tomato Soup

Cooking time 19 [13½] minutes Serves 4

1	*onion, chopped*	*1*
1	*clove garlic, chopped*	*1*
50 g	*butter*	*2 oz*
600 ml	*stock*	*1 pint*
675 g	*tomatoes, roughly chopped*	*1½ lb*
	salt and pepper	
	pinch of sugar	

Combine the onion, garlic and butter in a deep dish, cover and cook on high for 3 [2] minutes. Add 300 ml/½ pint of the stock and tomatoes. Cover with a lid and cook on high for 6[4] minutes. Then reduce the setting to medium high and cook for 8 [6] minutes. Puree the mixture in a food processor or blender and sieve to remove the tomato skins. Add the remaining stock and season. Reheat on high for 2[1½] minutes.

Cream of Watercress Soup

Cooking time 13-15 [9½-11½] minutes Serves 6-8

225 g	*watercress — washed and picked over*	*8 oz*
50 g	*butter*	*2 oz*
50 g	*plain flour*	*2 oz*
1.15 litres	*chicken stock*	*2 pints*
1 tbsp	*lemon juice*	*1 tbsp*
150 ml	*double cream*	*5 fl oz*
2	*egg yolks*	*2*
	salt and freshly ground pepper	

Heat butter in a deep glass dish on High for 60 [40] seconds. Blend in flour and gradually add 1½ pint stock. Cook on High for 10-12 [7-8½] minutes until the sauce has thickened, stirring occasionally. Season with salt and pepper, whisk in lemon juice, egg yolks and cream.

Meanwhile pour remaining half-pint liquid into a blender or processor, turn machine on and gradually add watercress, reserving a few leaves for decorations. Add to sauce and heat on High for 2-3 [1½-2] minutes.

Serve garnished with watercress.

Easy

Vegetable Soup

Cooking time 20 [14] minutes Serves 4

25 g	*butter*	*1 oz*
100 g	*potato, peeled and diced*	*4 oz*
100 g	*carrot, peeled and diced*	*4 oz*
1	*onion, chopped*	*1*
1	*leek, finely sliced*	*1*
½	*red pepper, cored, deseeded and diced*	*½*
900 ml	*chicken stock, hot*	*1½ pints*
	salt and pepper	
	bouquet garni	

Place the butter, potato, carrot, onion, and leek in a large dish. Cover and cook on high for 10 [7] minutes, stirring halfway through the cooking. Stir in hot chicken stock, salt, pepper and bouquet garni. Cover and cook on high for 10(7) minutes, stirring again halfway through cooking. Adjust the seasoning and discard the bouquet garni. Serve with lots of crusty bread.

Microtip

When cooking eggs in the microwave, it is important to prick the yolks very lightly to make sure they do not burst during cooking.

Timings given are for 650 [750-800] watt ovens

Tomato Soup page 16
Cream of Watercress Soup page 16
Vegetable Soup page 16

Easy

Marinated Mushrooms

Cooking time 10 [7] minutes Serves 4

6	*rashers rindless bacon — chopped*	*6*
225 g	*mushrooms — sliced*	*8 oz*
2 tbsp	*oil*	*2 tbsp*
2	*cloves garlic — crushed*	*2*
175 ml	*red wine*	*6 fl oz*
	seasoning	
1 tbsp	*freshly chopped parsley*	*1 tbsp*

Cook chopped bacon and oil in a dish on High for 3 [2] minutes. Stir in the garlic and mushrooms and cook on High for 2 [1½] minutes. Stir well. Add the red wine and cook uncovered for 5 [3½] minutes. Season to taste. Cover and leave to cool. Chill.

To garnish, sprinkle with chopped parsley and serve with crusty bread.

Mushroom and Egg Cocottes

Cooking time 4-5 [3-4] minutes Serves 4

25 g	*butter*	*1 oz*
4	*eggs*	*4*
100 g	*mushrooms, sliced*	*4 oz*
	salt and pepper	
4 tbsp	*double cream*	*4 tbsp*
	paprika	

Butter four ramekin dishes and break an egg into each one. Pierce the yolks with the point of a knife or a cocktail stick.

Combine the butter and mushrooms together in a bowl and cook uncovered on high for 60 [40] seconds. Stir well and season to taste. Reserve a few slices of mushroom for garnish and spoon the rest over the eggs. Spoon the cream over the mushrooms and sprinkle with a little paprika. Cook on high for 3-4 [2-3] minutes and stand for 3-4 minutes. Garnish with the reserved mushroom slices and serve hot with fingers of toast.

Haddock in Prawn Sauce

Cooking time 8-8½ [5½-6] minutes Serves 4 as a starter

225 g	*haddock*	*8 oz*
250 ml	*milk*	*8 fl oz*
15 g	*margarine*	*½ oz*
15 g	*plain flour*	*½ oz*
50 g	*prawns*	*2 oz*
	salt and pepper	
½ level tsp	*dried mustard*	*½ level tsp*
2 tsp	*lemon juice*	*2 tsp*
1 level tsp	*Worcester sauce*	*1 level tsp*
	creamed potato	
	chopped parsley for garnish	

Lay fish in a dish and pour over 3 tablespoons of milk, cover and cook on high for 3 [2] minutes. Stand for 2 minutes then drain liquid into reserved milk. Flake and bone fish and divide between four individual dishes, already piped with creamed potato.

Melt margarine in bowl on high for 30 [20] seconds and stir in flour. Blend in the milk and fish juices gradually and cook on high for 3 [2] minutes, stirring twice during cooking. Add mustard, lemon juice, Worcester sauce and seasoning to taste. Stir in prawns and pour over fish. Reheat on high for 1½-2 [1-1½] minutes. Serve sprinkled with freshly chopped parsley.

Easy

Pork and Orange Pate

Cooking time 25 [17] minutes Serves 8

225 g	*belly pork — derinded*	*8 oz*
225 g	*lean pork — derinded*	*8 oz*
75 g	*smoked bacon rashers — derinded*	*3 oz*
50 g	*fresh breadcrumbs*	*2 oz*
1	*onion — chopped*	*1*
1	*clove garlic — crushed*	*1*
	rind and juice of one orange	
1 tbsp	*sherry*	*1 tbsp*
	salt and pepper	

Finely chop or process the pork and bacon. Combine all ingredients together and press into a 900 ml/1½ pint oblong container. Cover with cooking film and shield across each corner with a strip of foil. Cook on Medium High for 25 [17]* minutes. Leave to cool. Garnish with orange slices and bay leaves.

* For 800 watt oven cook on Medium High for 15 minutes.

Easy

Savoury Mushrooms

Cooking time 4-5 [3-3½] minutes Serves 4

8	*cup mushrooms, with stems*	*8*
1 oz	*butter*	*25 g*
1 oz	*breadcrumbs*	*25 g*
1 oz	*Stilton cheese, crumbled*	*25 g*
	chopped parsley to garnish	

Chop the mushroom stems and cook them with the butter, uncovered on High for 2 [1½] minutes. Stir in the breadcrumbs and cheese, and press the mixture into mushroom caps. Arrange on serving plate and cook, covered, on High for 2-3 [1½-2] minutes. Serve hot, sprinkled with a little chopped parsley.

Country Pate

Cooking time 7½-8½ [5½-6] minutes Serves 8

1	*medium onion, chopped*	*1*
1	*clove garlic, crushed*	*1*
50 g	*butter*	*2 oz*
100 g	*chicken livers, chopped*	*4 oz*
100 g	*rindless pork belly, chopped*	*4 oz*
4	*rashers rindless streaky bacon, chopped*	*4*
2 tbsp	*brandy*	*2 tbsp*
2 tbsp	*cream*	*2 tbsp*
	salt and pepper	
1	*bay leaf to garnish*	*1*

Combine the onion, garlic and 25g/1 oz of the butter in a bowl, cover and cook on high for 2-3 [1½-2] minutes until the onion is soft. Add the livers, pork and bacon. Cook on high for 5 [3½] minutes, stirring twice during cooking. Process the mixture in a liquidiser or food processor until smooth. Add the brandy, cream and seasoning to taste. Turn the mixture into a suitable serving dish; smooth the top. Melt the remaining 25 g/1 oz butter on high for 30 [20] seconds and pour it over pate; garnish with the bay leaf. Chill before serving.

Easy

Hot Grapefruit

Cooking time 1½-2 [1-1½] minutes Serves 2

1	*large grapefruit*	*1*
25 g	*demerara sugar*	*1 oz*

Cut the grapefuit in half and loosen around flesh. Remove pips and loosen each segment. Sprinkle the sugar over each half and place them in two dishes. Cook on high for 1½-2 [1-1½] minutes. Serve immediately.

Timings given are for 650 [750-800] watt ovens

FISH

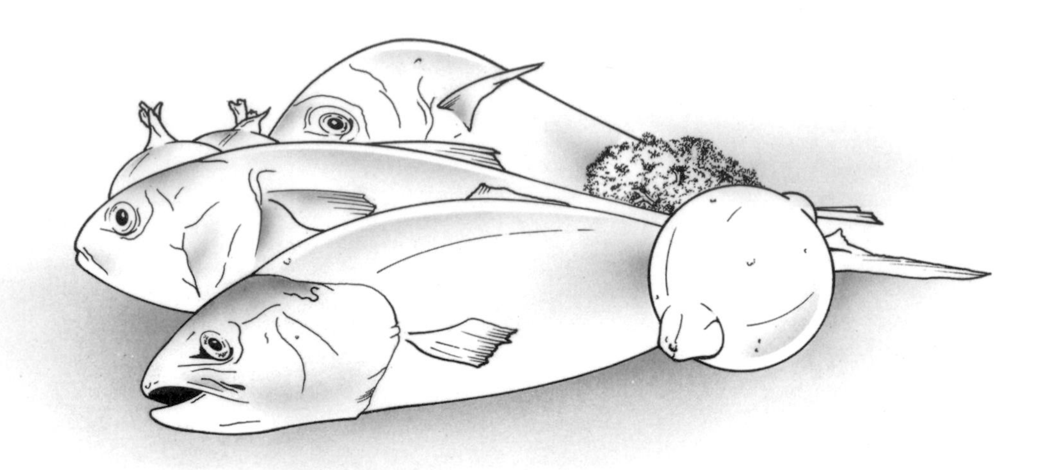

The microwave oven can cope with frozen fish, fresh fish, boil-in-the-bag fish, fish in sauce, in fact most methods of cooking fish with the exception of frying.

Fish can be cooked thawed or from frozen with just some melted butter and a little lemon juice. To test if fish is cooked, the centre should be just firm enough to flake. Whole fish, up to 450 g/1 lb can be cooked on high power. For whole fish over 450 g/1 lb start on high but complete cooking on medium power. Protect the heads and tails with a small piece of foil, or tuck the tails under the body. Large, whole fish can be arranged in a curved dish to enable it to fit in the oven.

Breaded fish can be successfully cooked in the microwave by brushing with melted butter before cooking, although the finished results will not be as crisp.

When making a complete meal in the microwave, cook the fish last as vegetables hold their heat longer than fish. When reheating cooked fish use Medium power.

Trout with Broccoli and Mushrooms page 22

FISH

COOKING FISH

Food	Time on High per 450 g/1 lb	Method and Standing Time
Fish fillets	6 [4] minutes	Lay in baking dish with thickest part towards the outside. Brush with melted butter if desired and cover. Stand 3 minutes
Fish steaks	4 [3] minutes	As above. Turn steaks over half-way through and brush with butter. Stand 3 minutes
Flat fish	3 [2]minutes	Arrange in baking dish with thin end tucked underneath to prevent overcooking. Cover. Stand 3 minutes
Whole fish	4 [3] minutes	When cooking several fish together, lay them head to tail. Make slits in skin to prevent bursting. Cover. Stand 3 minutes
Whole fish over 450 g/1 lb	8 [6] minutes on Medium High per 450 g/1 lb	Shield head and tail with a little foil, lay or curve into a dish. Cover. Stand 5-10 minutes

For those ovens with 'weight cook' just programme in the weight of the fish and press start. The oven will calculate the cooking time and the power level for you.

Trout with Broccoli and Mushrooms *Easy*

Cooking time 22 [14] minutes Serves 4

4	trout — cleaned and gutted	4
225 g	broccoli	8 oz
50 g	butter	2 oz
2	spring onions — sliced	2
100 g	mushrooms — sliced	4 oz
1 tbsp	lemon juice	1 tbsp
1 tbsp	freshly chopped parsley	1 tbsp
	salt	
25 g	toasted breadcrumbs	1 oz

Arrange fish in shallow dish alternating head to tail. Cover and cook on high for 12 [7] minutes. Leave to stand. Arrange broccoli with 2-3 tablespoons water in a covered dish and cook on high for 5 [4] minutes. Melt 25 g/1 oz butter in a separate bowl on high for 40 [30] seconds. Stir in onion and mushrooms. Cover and cook on high for 3 [2] minutes. Stir in parsley, lemon juice and a little salt.

Remove fish to a serving plate, arrange drained broccoli arround fish and spoon mushrooms over. In the mushroom bowl melt the remaining 25 g/1 oz butter on high for 60 [40] seconds and stir in breadcrumbs and scatter over mushrooms, serve immediately.

Trout with Almonds *Easy*

Cooking Time 16 [10½] minutes Serves 4

4	medium trout — gutted but left whole	4
	a little lemon juice	
	salt and pepper	
50 g	flaked almonds	2 oz
50 g	butter	2 oz

Sprinkle inside the body cavities with lemon juice, salt and pepper.

Arrange fish in a large shallow dish alternating head to tail for even cooking. Cover and cook on high for 12 [8] minutes. Leave fish to stand while preparing almonds.

Combine butter and almonds in a bowl, cover and cook on high for 4 [2½] minutes. Stir them well and spoon over fish. Garnish with sprigs of parsley to serve.

For 2 servings: Cook fish for 8 [5½] minutes and almonds for 2½ [2] minutes.

Timings given are for 650 [750-800] watt ovens

Easy

Oriental Fish

Cooking time 10 [7] minutes Serves 4

750 g	white fish eg cod or haddock	1½ lbs
25 g	butter	1 oz
4	spring onions — sliced	4
1	clove garlic — crushed	1
1 tsp	grated fresh ginger	1 tsp
1 tbsp	sugar	1 tbsp
1 tbsp	wine vinegar	1 tbsp
2 tbsp	soy sauce	2 tbsp
3 level tsp	cornflour	3 level tsp
5 tbsp	water	5 tbsp
	whole prawns for garnish (optional)	

Lay fish in a shallow dish, cover and cook on high for 6 [4] minutes. Leave to stand. In a separate bowl combine butter, spring onions (reserve a few pieces of green for garnish), garlic and ginger, cover and cook on high for 2 [1½] minutes. Stir in sugar, wine vinegar and soy sauce.

Blend cornflour with water and mix to a smooth paste, stir into sauce. Cook uncovered on high for 2 [1½] minutes. Stir well.

Drain juices from fish into sauce then pour sauce over fish. Garnish with reserved pieces of spring onion and whole prawns if used.

For 2 servings: Cook fish 4-5 [3] minutes, onions for 80 [60] seconds, sauce 80 [60] seconds.

Microtip

Plates can be warmed by placing under a dish being cooked or reheated in the microwave. The conduction of heat will then warm the plates.

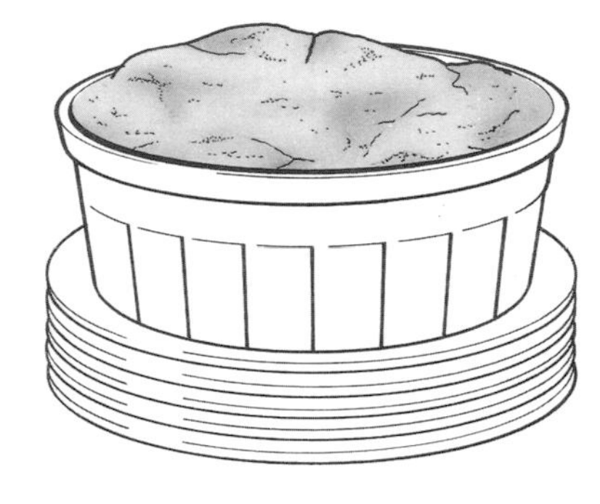

Easy

Haddock Fillets with Oregano

Cooking time 6 [4½] minutes Serves 2-3

350 g	haddock fillet	12 oz
1 tbsp	water	1 tbsp
25 g	butter	1 oz
1 tsp	oregano	1 tsp
25g	fresh breadcrumbs	1 oz
1 tbsp	seedless raisins	1 tbsp
4	slices lemon	4
	salt and pepper	

Lay fish in a shallow dish. Add water and dot with butter. Mix oregano with breadcrumbs and sprinkle over fish. Cover and cook on high 4 [3] minutes. Scatter over raisins. Arrange lemon slices on fish, season to taste, re-cover and cook a further 2 [1½] minutes on high. Stand 3 minutes.

Easy

Fish in Mushroom Sauce

Cooking time 9-11 [6-8] minutes Serves 4

450 g	haddock or cod	1 lb
1	small onion, chopped	1
1 tbsp	oil	1 tbsp
1 (290 g)	can condensed mushroom soup	1 (10½ oz)
1 tbsp	chopped parsley	1 tbsp
	salt and pepper	

Place the fish in a shallow dish with 2 tablespoons water. Cover and cook on high for 4-6 [3-4] minutes. Stand for 2 minutes. Drain, skin, bone and flake the fish. Combine the onion and oil, cover and cook on high for 3 [2] minutes. Add the soup and head on high for 2-3 [1½-2] minutes, stirring twice. Add the parsley, flaked fish and seasoning. Cook 1-2 minutes on high. Serve hot.

For 2 servings: Cook fish 3-4 [2-3] minutes, onion for 2 [1½] minutes and finally 40-60 seconds.

Timings given are for 650 [750-800] watt ovens

Paella page 25

Paella

Cooking time 18-20 [11½-13] minutes Serves 4

25 g	*butter*	*1 oz*
1	*onion, finely chopped*	*1*
1	*clove garlic, crushed*	*1*
½ tsp	*turmeric*	*½ tsp*
225 g	*long-grain rice*	*8 oz*
600 ml	*hot chicken stock*	*1 pint*
100 g	*cooked chicken, in chunks*	*4 oz*
100 g	*peeled prawns*	*4 oz*
75 g	*cooked mussels*	*3 oz*
50 g	*frozen peas*	*2 oz*
2	*tomatoes, skinned, deseeded and cut in strips*	*2*
	salt and pepper	
	whole prawns to garnish	

Combine the butter, onion and garlic and cook, covered, on high for 2 [1½-2] minutes. Add the turmeric, rice and stock and stir well. Cover and cook on high for 13 [8] minutes. Leave to stand for 5 minutes, for the rice to absorb the liquid.

Stir in the chicken, prawns, mussels, peas and tomato strips, season to taste. Cook uncovered on high for 3-4 [2-3] minutes, stirring occasionally. Serve hot garnished with whole prawns.

Sweet and Sour Prawns

Cooking time 11-12 [8] minutes Serves 4

75 g	*sugar*	*3 oz*
15 g	*cornflour*	*½ oz*
3 tbsp	*water*	*3 tbsp*
1 (225 g)	*can pineapple pieces drained, juice reserved*	*1 (8 oz)*
½	*green pepper, deseeded and chopped*	*½*
½	*red pepper, deseeded and chopped*	*½*
1	*clove garlic, crushed*	*1*
4 tbsp	*wine vinegar*	*4 tbsp*
3 tsp	*soy sauce*	*3 tsp*
450 g	*prawns*	*1 lb*

Blend the sugar and cornflour with the water. Add 4 tablespoons of the pineapple juice, peppers, garlic, vinegar and cook on high for 5-6 [4] minutes, stirring half-way through. Stand for 5 minutes, covered; add the pineapple pieces, soy sauce and prawns. Cover and heat through on high for 6 [4] minutes, stirring after 3 minutes. Serve hot with boiled rice. Garnish with spring onion curls.

For 2 servings: Cook sauce 3-4 [2½-3] minutes and heat through for 4 [3] minutes.

Microtip

Plates can also be warmed in the microwave by stacking them with a little water sprinkled between each one and microwaving on high. Two plates will take 60-90 [40-60] seconds and four plates will take 2 [1½] minutes.

Timings given are for 650 [750-800] watt ovens

Smoked Haddock in Sauce

Cooking time 13-14 [10-11] minutes Serves 4

350 g	*smoked haddock*	*12 oz*
300 ml	*milk*	*10 fl oz*
	bay leaf	
	salt and pepper	
1	*small onion, chopped*	*1*
25 g	*margarine*	*1 oz*
25 g	*plain flour*	*1 oz*
	pinch nutmeg pinch	
100 g	*frozen green beans, cooked and chopped*	*4 oz*

Lay the fish in a shallow dish. Add 4 tablespoons of the milk, the bay leaf, salt and pepper. Cover and cook on high for 4 [3] minutes until the fish flakes. Stand for 3 minutes.

Strain and reserve the cooking liquid; skin and flake the fish. Combine the onion and margarine and cook on high for 2 [1½] minutes. Add the flour and cook for 60 [40] seconds on high; blend in the rest of the milk and fish stock. Cook on high for 4-5 [3-4] minutes, stirring twice during cooking. Adjust the seasoning and stir in the nutmeg, fish and cooked beans. Heat on high for 2 [1½] minutes. Serve with cooked rice.

Lemon Stuffed Plaice Rolls

Cooking Time 12 [9] minutes Serves 4

8	*plaice fillets — skinned*	*8*
75 g	*breadcrumbs — fresh*	*3 oz*
	grated rind of 1 lemon	
2 tbsp	*chopped parsley*	*2 tbsp*
½ tsp	*mixed dried herbs*	*½ tsp*
25 g	*butter*	*1 oz*
	salt and pepper	
15 g	*cornflour*	*½ oz*
150 ml	*dry white wine*	*¼ pint*
150 ml	*milk*	*¼ pint*

Combine breadcrumbs, lemon rind, parsley, herbs and seasoning. Melt butter on high for 60 [40] seconds and bind breadcrumb mixture, add a little milk if necessary. Divide between fillets and roll each one up tightly. Arrange in a shallow dish and pour over the wine. Cover and cook on high for 8 [6] minutes. Leave to stand.

Blend the cornflour with a little milk to a smooth paste. Stir in remaining milk and juices from the fish. Cook on high for 3 [2] minutes, stirring halfway through cooking, season to taste. Pour sauce over fish and sprinkle with a little chopped parsley and decorate with lemon slices to serve.

NB Poach the plaice skins in the milk and cook on high for 3 [2] minutes and leave to stand while preparing the fish, drain liquid from skins and use as milk in the sauce.

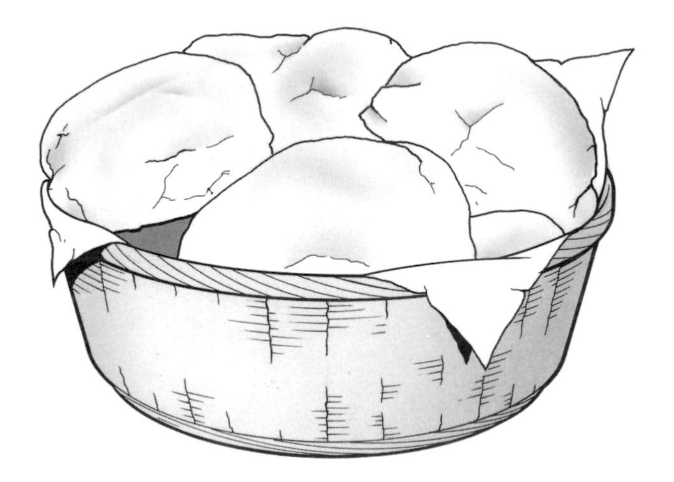

Microtip

Bread rolls can be warmed in a napkin-lined basket ready to serve. Half a dozen rolls will take 30 [20] seconds on high.

Timings given are for 650 [750-800] watt ovens

MEAT

Joints of meat will generally take about a third of the conventional cooking time when cooked by microwave. Do not salt the meat as it attracts moisture and has a toughening effect. The only exception to this is pork, when you do rub salt into the skin to produce crackling. Regular shaped joints cook the best and may be cooked in a roasting bag loosely closed with an elastic band or plastic clip or on a rack in a covered container. Most joints with a cooking time longer than 15 minutes will brown automatically otherwise sprinkle them with microwave seasoning or paprika pepper before cooking. Start cooking joints with the fat side down then turn them over. Larger joints need turning several times during cooking.

Most joints are better cooked on medium-high power, although gammon and bacon joints should be cooked on medium power. Allow 1 minute per pound weight of meat, extra for stuffed joints. Shield narrow areas, such as the end of the legs with a piece of foil, making sure that the foil does not touch the sides of the oven as the turntable rotates.

When cooking pork, for best results score the skin well then remove it and rub with a little oil. Sprinkle with salt then lay the skin back on top of the joint and cook together. Remove the rind and give it 2-3 minutes on high on its own after cooking to crispen it.

MEAT

When the meat is cooked, cover with foil, shiny side downwards, to retain the heat. Stand for 15-30 minutes before slicing.
Sausages, steaks, chops and burgers that require a grilled look need to be cooked in a special browning dish when cooked in those ovens without a browning facility or seared in a frying pan before cooking in the microwave.
Rashers of bacon can be cooked on a special microwave rack or across the top of an upturned cereal bowl, this allows the surplus fat to drain away. Cover the rashers lightly with kitchen paper to prevent splattering the inside of the oven.

ROASTING CHART

Meat	***Time per 450g/1lb***	***Standing Times***
Beef (Rare)	*6 [4] minutes on high* *8 [6] minutes on med high*	*When cooked, wrap in foil and stand 15-30 minutes*
Beef (Medium)	*7 [5] minutes on high* *9 [6½] minutes on med high*	*As above*
Beef (Well Done)	*8 [5½] minutes on high* *10½ [7] minutes on med high*	*As above*
Pork	*8-9 [5½-6] minutes high* *11 [7-8] minutes on med high*	*As above*
Lamb	*8-9 [5½-6] mins on high* *11 [7-8] mins on med high*	*As above*
Ham	*7 [5] minutes on high* *12 [8] minutes on medium*	*Stand for 15-20 minutes* *before serving or leave to cool — covered*
Chicken	*6 [4] minutes on high* *8 [6] minutes on med high*	*Stand for 15-20 minutes*
Turkey	*6 [4] minutes on high* *8 [4] minutes on med high*	*Stand for 15-20 minutes.* *For larger birds — start cooking breast side down and turn over halfway through cooking*
Duck	*7 [5] minutes on high* *9 [6½] minutes on med high*	*As for turkey*
Bacon Rashers 2 Rashers *4 Rashers* *6 Rashers* *8 Rashers*	*1½-2 [1-1½] minutes* *2½-3½ [2-2½] minutes* *5-6 [3½-4] minutes* *6½-7½ [4½-5] minutes*	*Arrange on rack and cover with absorbent kitchen paper.*

For those ovens with 'weight cook' just select meat category, programme in the weight and press start. The oven works out the cooking time and the power level for you.

Chilli Con Carne

Cooking time 22-23 [16½-17] minutes Serves 4

450 g	*lean minced beef*	*1 lb*
1	*large onion, chopped*	*1*
1	*clove garlic, crushed*	*1*
1 (400 g) can	*tomatoes*	*1 (14 oz) can*
1 tbsp	*tomato puree*	*1 tbsp*
1 tbsp	*mild chilli powder*	*1 tbsp*
1 tsp	*ground cumin*	*1 tsp*
1 tsp	*sugar*	*1 tsp*
1 tsp	*salt*	*1 tsp*
	pinch of pepper	
1 (425 g) can	*red kidney beans, drained and rinsed*	*1 (15 oz) can*

Put the beef into a casserole dish. Break it up with a fork. Add the onion and garlic. Cook on high for 5 [4] minutes, stirring once or twice to cook the meat evenly. Add the tomatoes, tomato puree and seasonings and stir well. Cover, and cook on high for 15 [11] minutes. Stir in the kidney beans. Cover the casserole again and cook on high for 2-3 [1½-2] minutes. Stand for 10 minutes for the flavour to develop. Serve with boiled rice. **For 2 servings:** Cook beef and onion for 3½ [2½] minutes then 10 [7] minutes and finally for 1½ [1] minutes.

Microtip

The shape of the dish can influence the cooking, round containers are best. Square or oblong dishes of food cook less evenly as the corners are likely to overcook. Small pieces of foil can be used to shield the corners.

Steak and Kidney Suet Pie

Cooking time 19½-21 [13½-14] minutes Serves 4

1	*large onion, chopped*	*1*
25 g	*margarine*	*1 oz*
450 g	*good stewing steak, cubed*	*1 lb*
175 g	*lamb's kidney, chopped*	*6 oz*
25 g	*plain flour*	*1 oz*
	salt and pepper	
1	*beef stock cube*	*1*
300 ml	*hot water*	*½ pint*
	Suet Pastry	
225 g	*self raising flour, sifted*	*8 oz*
	pinch of salt	
100 g	*shredded suet*	*4 oz*
2-3 tbsp	*dried mixed herbs (optional)*	*2-3 tbsp*
150 ml	*water*	*¼ pint*
1 tsp	*diluted gravy browning or soy sauce*	*1 tsp*

Combine the onion and margarine in a casserole dish. Cover and cook on high for 3 [2] minutes. Add the steak and kidney and stir well. Cover again and cook on high for 8 [6] minutes, stirring during the cooking. Sprinkle with the flour and stir well. Crumble in the stock cube and add the hot water with the salt and pepper. Cover and cook on high for 3-4 [2] minutes then reduce the power to medium for 40 [30] minutes. With a slotted spoon remove the steak and kidney to a pie dish with some of the gravy. Reserve the rest to serve with the pie.

To make the pastry, stir the suet into the sifted flour and salt. Add the herbs, if using, then mix with sufficient water to make a firm dough. Roll out to fit the shape of the pie and lift it on to the meat. Brush the pastry with the diluted gravy browning or soy sauce and cook on high for 4½-5 [3-3½] minutes. Stand for 10 minutes before serving.

Cottage Pie

Cooking time 26 [18½] minutes Serves 4

1	large onion, chopped	1
450 g	minced beef	1 lb
25 g	plain flour	1 oz
1 tsp	dried mixed herbs	1 tsp
	salt and pepper	
1	beef stock cube	1
300 ml	hot water	½ pint
900 g	cooked mashed potatoes	2 lb
1 tbsp	toasted breadcrumbs	1 tbsp

Place the onion in a covered casserole and cook on high for 3 [2] minutes. Add the minced beef, breaking it up with a wooden spoon. Cook, uncovered on high for 5 [3½] minutes, stirring it twice during cooking. Sprinkle with the flour and herbs. Crumble the stock cube, stir well. Blend in the hot water and cook, covered on high for 15 [11] minutes. Stir well and carefully spread the mashed potato over the surface. Press it down with the back of a fork. Sprinkle with the toasted breadcrumbs and cook, uncovered, on high for 3 [2] minutes. Stand for 5 minutes before serving.

For 2 servings: Cook meat for 3½ [2½] minutes then 10 [7] minutes and finally for 2 [1½] minutes.

Cider Beef

Cooking time 49 [37] minutes Serves 4

½	green pepper, chopped	½
2	medium onions, sliced	2
25 g	margarine	1 oz
675 g	silverside beef, cubed	1½ lb
25 g	plain flour	1 oz
1	bay leaf	1
½ tsp	mixed herbs	½ tsp
½ tsp	dried oregano	½ tsp
1 tbsp	tomato puree	1 tbsp
150 ml	dry cider	5 fl oz
150 ml	beef stock	5 fl oz
	salt and pepper	

Combine onions, green pepper and margarine in casserole, cover and cook on high for 4 [3] minutes. Add beef, stir well, recover and cook on high for 5 [4] minutes, stir once during cooking.

Sprinkle the flour over the meat and stir in together with all remaining ingredients. Cover and cook on power level medium low for 40 [30] minutes. Stir halfway through cooking. Leave to stand for 10 minutes before serving.

Easy

Beef Stew

Cooking time 42-52 [30½-38½] minutes Serves 4

1	medium onion, sliced	1
2	carrots, sliced	2
25 g	margarine	1 oz
675 g	good braising steak, cubed	1½ lb
1 tsp	dried mixed herbs	1 tsp
1 tbsp	plain flour	1 tbsp
300 ml	beef stock	½ pint
	salt and pepper	
1 tsp	gravy browning (optional)	1 tsp

Combine the onion, carrots and margarine in a casserole dish. Cover and cook on high for 5 [3½] minutes. Stir well and add the cubed steak and herbs. Cover and cook on high for 7 [5] minutes, stirring halfway through cooking to distribute the heat. Sprinkle with the flour and stir well. Blend in the stock and seasoning and add the gravy browning for a rich colour. Cover, and cook for 30 [22] minutes on medium or 40 [30] minutes on medium low. Stand for 10 minutes before serving.

This casserole will benefit from leaving to go cold and reheating later in the day (or next day).

Steak Parcels

Cooking time 9-10 [6½-7] minutes Serves 4

2×225 g	rump steaks (or fillet or sirloin)	2×8 oz
75 g	fresh white breadcrumbs	3 oz
50 g	butter	2 oz
1	medium onion, chopped	1
3 tbsp	freshly chopped parsley	3 tbsp
1 tsp	dried thyme	1 tsp
50 g	mushrooms, sliced	2 oz
	salt and pepper	
3-4 tsp	made mustard	3-4 tsp
4½ tbsp	beef stock (dissolve ½ stock cube)	3 fl oz

Lay steaks in a large polythene bag and flatten with a rolling pin or mallet. Cut each into 2 giving 4 pieces.

Combine half butter with onion and cook on high for 2-3 [1½-2] minutes. Stir in parsley, thyme and mushrooms and breadcrumbs.

Spread flattened steaks with made mustard and sprinkle with seasoning. Divide stuffing between steaks and spread flat. Roll up and secure with cocktail sticks.

Arrange in a shallow dish with the join underneath. Sprinkle with pepper and dot with remaining half of butter and spoon over beef stock. Cover and cook on high for 7 [5] minutes. Stand for 5 minutes. Serve each roll sliced on individual plates with juices spooned over.

For 2 servings: Cook onion for 1½ [1] minutes then steaks 4 [3] minutes.

Beef Bourguignonne

Cooking time 46 [30½- 33½] minutes Serves 4

1	large onion, chopped	1
175 g	carrots, chopped	6 oz
2	rashers rindless bacon, chopped	2
675 g	topside or sirloin beef	1½ lb
175 g	mushrooms, sliced	6 oz
25 g	plain flour	1 oz
	salt and pepper	
150 ml	beef stock	5 fl oz
150 ml	red wine	5 fl oz
1-2 tbsp	brandy	1-2 tbsp
	grated rind of ½ orange	
1	bouquet garni	1

Combine the onion, carrots and bacon in a casserole, cover and microwave on high for 5 [3½] minutes. Cut the meat into narrow strips about 2.5-5 cm/1-2 in long. Add these to the casserole, stir and cover. Cook on high for 7 [4-5] minutes, stirring halfway through cooking. Stir in the mushrooms and sprinkle with the flour. Stir again, then blend in remaining ingredients, cover and cook on high for 4 [3] minutes then on medium power for 30 [20-22] minutes. Stand for 10 minutes. Serve with boiled rice.

For 2 servings: Cook vegetables for 3½ [2½] minutes. Cook meat 4½ [3] minutes then finally for 2½ [2] minutes and 20 [12-14] minutes on medium power.

Microtip

During cooking, food has to be stirred to redistribute the heat. Move items inwards from the edge of a casserole or dish.

Timings given are for 650 [750-800] watt ovens

Meatballs in Tomato Sauce

Cooking time 20 [15] minutes Serves 4

450 g	lean minced beef	1 lb
225 g	sausage meat	8 oz
50 g	fresh breadcrumbs	2 oz
1	small onion, finely chopped	1
2 tbsp	freshly chopped parsley	2 tbsp
½ tsp	salt	½ tsp
¼ tsp	pepper	¼ tsp
¼ tsp	nutmeg	¼ tsp
2	small beaten eggs	2
	Tomato Sauce	
40 g	butter	1½ oz
100 g	mushrooms, chopped	4 oz
40 g	plain flour	1½ oz
1 tbsp	tomato puree	1 tbsp
150 ml	hot beef stock	¼ pint
400g can	of tomatoes	14 oz can
	salt and pepper	

Combine all the ingredients for the meat balls and form into 16 balls. Arrange in a large shallow dish and cook uncovered on high for 4 [3] minutes. Turn each one over and continue to cook on high for 4 [3] minutes, cover and set aside while making sauce.

For the sauce, combine butter and mushrooms in a bowl and cook on high for 2 [1½] minutes, stir in the flour, tomato puree, hot stock and mix well, stir in the tomatoes and juice, season to taste, cover and cook on high for 8 [5½] minutes.

Liquidise in a blender or food processor until smooth, then pour over meat balls. Reheat 2 minutes on high. Serve with cooked noodles.

Stir-Fried Steak with Peppers

Cooking time 11½ [8] minutes Serves 4

1½ level tbsp	cornflour	1½ level tbsp
3 tbsp	soy sauce	3 tbsp
1 tbsp	white wine vinegar	1 tbsp
1	beef stock cube, crumbled	1
½ tsp	sugar	½ tsp
½ tsp	ground ginger	½ tsp
1	clove garlic, crushed	1
¼ tsp	pepper	¼ tsp
1 tbsp	oil	1 tbsp
1	green pepper, deseeded and thinly sliced	1
1	red pepper, deseeded and thinly sliced	1
1	medium onion, thinly sliced	1
675 g	beef sirloin or grilling steak, cut into 2.5 cm/1 in strips	1½ lb
100 g	button mushrooms	4 oz
	chopped parsley, (optional)	

Place the cornflour in a small bowl and mix to a smooth paste with the soy sauce, wine vinegar, crumbled stock cube, sugar, ginger, garlic and pepper and leave aside.

Combine the oil, peppers and onion in a large dish. Cover and cook on high for 5 [3½] minutes. Stir in the beef and cook, uncovered, on high for 5 [3½] minutes, stirring halfway through the cooking. Add the sauce to the beef with the mushrooms and stir well. Continue to cook on high for 90 [60] seconds. Serve hot, sprinkled with a little chopped parsley, if desired.

For 2 servings: Cook onion for 3½ [2½] minutes, cook beef for 3½ [2½] minutes and finally for 40 [30] seconds.

Stir-Fried Steak with Peppers page 32

Easy

Beefburgers with Pizza Sauce

Cooking time 15 [11] minutes Serves 4

450 g	minced lean beef	1 lb
1 tsp	oregano	1 tsp
1	onion, chopped	1
	salt and pepper	
	Pizza Sauce	
15 g	margarine	½ oz
1	small onion, chopped	1
½	green pepper, deseeded and chopped	½
50 g	mushrooms, sliced	2 oz
1 (400 g) can	mushrooms, chopped	1 (14 oz) can
½ tsp	oregano	½ tsp
	salt and pepper	

Combine the beefburger ingredients, mix well and form into 8 burgers. Pre-heat an empty browning dish on high for 7 [5] minutes or according to manufacturers instructions. Quickly place the burgers on the dish and cook on high for 2 [1½] minutes on each side. Keep them warm, while making the sauce.

To make the sauce, cook the onion with the margarine on high for 2 [1½] minutes. Add the remaining ingredients and cook on high for 4 [3] minutes, stirring once during cooking. Pour the sauce over the beefburgers and serve hot.

Midweek Pie

Easy

Cooking time 11-13 [8-9½] minutes Serves 4

1	medium onion chopped	1
1 tbsp	oil	1 tbsp
15 g	flour	½ oz
300 ml	stock	½ pint
1 tbsp	tomato puree	1 tbsp
	salt and pepper	
½ tsp	mixed herbs	½ tsp
350 g	cooked pork or lamb, chopped or minced	12 oz
350 g	cooked potato, mashed	12 oz
50 g	grated cheese	2 oz
½ tsp	mixed herbs	½ tsp
2 tbsp	toasted breadcrumbs	2 tbsp

Combine the onion and oil and cook on high for 3 [2] minutes until the onion is soft. Stir in the flour and cook for 60 [40] seconds on high. Blend in the stock, tomato puree, seasoning and mixed herbs. Cook on high for 3-4 [2-3] minutes stirring twice during cooking. Add the meat and stir well. Smooth the top and cover with the potato. Combine the cheese, herbs and breadcrumbs and sprinkle the mixture over the potato. Cook on high for 4-5 [3-3½] minutes. Stand for 5 minutes.

For 2 servings: Cook onion for 2 [1½] minutes, sauce for 2-3 [1½-2] minutes and finally 3½ [2½] minutes.

Piquant Lamb Chops

Easy

Cooking time 12 [8½] minutes Serves 4

8	best end of neck lamb chops	8
4 tbsp	red wine	4 tbsp
2	cloves garlic, crushed	2
1 tsp	dried marjoram	1 tsp
2 tbsp	chopped fresh parsley	2 tbsp
1 tbsp	drained capers, chopped	2 tbsp
	salt and pepper	
1 tbsp	lemon juice	1 tbsp
2 tbsp	yoghurt or single cream	2 tbsp

In a large shallow dish, combine the red wine, garlic, marjoram, parsley, capers, salt and pepper and stir well.

Lay the chops in the marinade, coating well each side, cover and leave for 2 hours, turning half way. Turn chops once more, cover and cook in marinade, on high for 10 [6-7] minutes. Drain juices from chops into a bowl, stir in lemon juice and cook on high for 2 [1½] minutes, stir in yoghurt or cream and pour over chops. Sprinkle with a little chopped parsley and serve hot.

For 2 servings: Cook chops for 6 [4] minutes and juices for 90 [60] seconds.

Timings given are for 650 [750-800] watt ovens

Loin of Lamb with Redcurrant Sauce

Cooking time 32-35 [26] minutes Serves 4-6

1	onion, finely chopped	1
1	clove garlic, crushed	1
1 tbsp	chopped fresh parsley	1 tbsp
½ tsp	dried marjoram	½ tsp
½ tsp	dried rosemary	½ tsp
	grated rind and juice of ½ lemon	
75 g	pork sausagemeat	3 oz
25 g	fresh breadcrumbs	1 oz
	salt and pepper	
1-2 tbsp	milk	1-2 tbsp
1.5 kg	loin of lamb, boned	3 lb
	Redcurrant Sauce	
25 g	butter	1 oz
25 g	plain flour	1 oz
300 ml	chicken or vegetable stock	½ pint
2 tbsp	redcurrant jelly	2 tbsp
	grated rind and juice of ½ lemon	
	grated rind and juice of 1 small orange	
1 tsp	chopped fresh mint	1 tsp

Combine the onion, garlic, herbs, lemon, sausagemeat and breadcrumbs. Season to taste and moisten with milk. Spread the stuffing in pockets of the boned meat. Roll it up and tie with string. Score the surface of the meat with a sharp knife. Place it on a rack, cover and cook on medium high power for 27 [22] minutes. Remove from the oven and wrap the meat in foil. Leave to stand for 20-30 minutes before serving.

To make the sauce, melt the butter on high for 40 seconds. Blend in the stock, jelly, rind and juices and cook on high for 4-5 [3] minutes, stirring twice during cooking. Stir in the mint and serve with the sliced meat.

Stir-fried Pork with Pineapple Sauce

Cooking time 15-17 [12-13] minutes Serves 4

150 ml	water	5 fl oz
1½ tbsp	cornflour	1½ tbsp
1 (225 g) can	pineapple pieces, drained, juice preserved	1 (8 oz) can
1 tbsp	tomato ketchup	1 tbsp
2 tsp	soy sauce	2 tsp
2 tsp	sugar	2 tsp
1	small onion, chopped	1
½	crumbled chicken stock cube	½
¼ tsp	ground ginger	¼ tsp
450 g	boned pork loin, cut in narrow strips	1 lb
250 g	celery, sliced	9 oz
1	green pepper, deseeded and cut into thin sticks	1
150 g	carrots, cut into thin sticks	5 oz
100 g	mushrooms, sliced	4 oz
2 tbsp	oil	2 tbsp

Blend the water into the cornflour and add 4½ tablespoons of the pineapple juice, the drained pineapple pieces, ketchup, soy sauce, onion, stock cube and ginger. Cook on high for 5-6 [3½-4] minutes, stirring twice during cooking. Set aside.

Combine the pork, celery, green pepper and carrots in a casserole dish. Cook uncovered on high for 8 [7] minutes, stirring several times during cooking to distribute the heat. Stir in the mushrooms and the pineapple sauce. Cook on high for 2-3 [1½-2] minutes and serve hot with cooked noodles or plain boiled rice.

For 2 servings: Cook sauce 3½ [2½] minutes, cook meat and vegetables for 5 [3½] minutes and finally for 1½ [1] minutes.

Timings given are for 650 [750-800] watt ovens

Beefburgers with Pizza Sauce page 34

Apricot Stuffed Pork page 38

Apricot Stuffed Pork

Cooking time 33 [24] minutes Serves 8-12

1½ kg	loin of pork — boned	3 lb
75 g	liver pate	3 oz
10-12	no-soak apricots	10-12
1 tbsp	chopped fresh parsley	1 tbsp
½ tsp	origanum	½ tsp
	salt and pepper	
2	carrots, sliced	2
1	onion, sliced	1
150 ml	stock or water	¼ pint
1	bay leaf	1
2 tbsp	toasted breadcrumbs	2 tbsp

Lay pork, skin side down on dish, spread with pate. Lay apricots on pate in single layer, sprinkle with parsley, origanum, salt and pepper. Roll up firmly and tie to prevent it opening when cooking.

Combine carrots, onions, stock and bay leaf in base of dish. Place pork on top, cover and cook on medium high for 33 [24]* minutes.

Lift Pork from vegetables and juices (use these for soup or puree and use in a sauce or gravy). Remove skin from pork and coat the fat with the toasted breadcrumbs. Leave to go cold.

Serve sliced with a green salad or as part of a buffet table.

* For 800 watt oven — cook for 22 minutes on medium high. Leave to stand 15 minutes.

Easy

Glazed Ham

Cooking Time 12 [8] minutes per 450g/1 lb

	Gammon joint soaked overnight	
3 tbsp	redcurrant jelly	3 tbsp
½ tsp	ground ginger	½ tsp

Weigh joint and calculate cooking time of 12 [8] minutes per 450 g/1lb, to be cooked on medium power. Place on microwave rack or upturned shallow dish, cover and cook for half the time calculated on medium power.

Remove cover, cut away the rind and discard. Turn joint over and score the fat in a diamond pattern. Mix the ginger with the redcurrant jelly and brush over the fat. Cover and cook for second half of cooking time, again on medium power.

Leave to stand 15-20 minutes before serving hot. Alternatively leave to go cold.

Sweet-and-Sour Gammon Steaks Easy

Cooking Time 17-19 [12-14] minutes Serves 4

4 (450 g)	gammon steaks	4 (1 lb)
	Sweet and Sour Sauce	
2	medium carrots, cut in fine strips	2
1	green pepper, deseeded and sliced	1
300 ml	cider	10 fl oz
2 tbsp	cornflour	2 tbsp
25 g	brown sugar	1 oz
1 (350g) can	pineapple pieces, drained juice reserved	1 (12oz) can
1 tbsp	clear honey	1 tbsp
1 tbsp	mustard pickle	1 tbsp
3 tsp	soy sauce	3 tsp

Place the gammon steaks on a rack. Cover with absorbent kitchen paper and cook on high for 6-7 [4-5] minutes. For the sauce, combine the carrot strips, pepper and cider and cook in a covered dish on high for 8 [6] minutes. Blend the cornflour and sugar with 150 ml/¼ pint of the pineapple juice and stir this into the vegetables. Add the remaining ingredients and cook on high for 3-4 [2-3] minutes, stirring twice during cooking. Serve hot with the gammon steaks.

For 2 servings: Cook gammon 3½-4 [2½] minutes and cook vegetables for 5 [3] minutes then sauce 2 [1½] minutes.

Timings given are for 650 [750-800] watt ovens

POULTRY

Whilst the standard microwave will not produce a crisp, brown skin that you will have with your conventional oven, it will more than reward you with a superb flavour and a moist and tender flesh.
Browning can be achieved artificially by brushing with melted butter, or diluted soy sauce or yeast extract and sprinkling with paprika pepper or microwave seasonings before cooking.
Microwaves with special browning facilities i.e. Grills, Convection, Halogen etc can be programmed to cook using the speed of microwaves plus the direct heat for conventional browning.
It is important to defrost all poultry completely before cooking. Boned poultry is particularly good cooked in the microwave as it is a compact shape. With the irregular shape of poultry, it is often advisable to shield the wings and leg bones with a small piece of foil. Make sure that they are not touching the walls of the oven as the turntable rotates.
Most chicken dishes are cooked on high power as are whole birds up to about 1.5 kg/3 lbs. Larger birds are better started on high for half the cooking time and finished on a lower setting. Start cooking larger birds breast-side down and turn over half-way through cooking or turn several times. Duck, goose and pheasant give better results cooked on medium power throughout cooking to prevent them drying out. If poultry is stuffed, allow 60 [40] seconds per 450 g/1 lb weight of bird extra cooking time. To check if it is cooked, pierce the bird between the leg and the body and when the juices are no longer pink the bird is cooked.

POULTRY

You may wish to finish cooking a chicken in a conventional oven to achieve a crisp skin. If so, allow 5-6 [4] minutes per 450 g/1 lb on high in the microwave oven and finish in a very hot conventional oven (240C, 475F, gas 9) for 15-30 minutes. For turkeys, allow 6-7 [5] minutes per 450 g/1 lb on medium high and finish in a moderately hot conventional oven (220C, 400F, gas 6).
The maximum size of turkey that can be satisfactorily cooked in your microwave is as follows:-
0.6 and 1.0 cu ft ovens - up to 4.5 kg/10 lb
1.2 and 1.3 cu ft ovens - up to 6.25 kg/14 lb

ROASTING CHART

Food	***Time***	***Standing Time***
Chicken	*6 [4] minutes per 450 g/ 1 lb on high 8 [6] minutes per 450 g/1 lb on med high*	*Stand for 15-20 minutes*
Turkey	*6 [4] minutes per 450 g/ 1 lb on high 8 [6] minutes per 450 g/ 1 lb on med high*	*Stand for 15-30 minutes. For larger birds, start cooking breast side down and turn over halfway through cooking*
Duck/pheasant/ goose	*7 [5] minutes per 450 g/ 1 lb on high 12 [8] minutes per 450 g/1 lb on medium*	*As for turkey. Stand 15-20 minutes*

For those ovens with 'weight cook', just programme the weight of the chicken and press start. The oven will work out the cooking time and power level for you.

Chicken Chow Mein 

Cooking time 11-12 [8-8½] minutes Serves 4

40 g	*margarine*	*1½ oz*
1	*small onion, chopped*	*1*
1	*green pepper, chopped*	*1*
1	*red pepper, chopped*	*1*
2	*celery sticks, chopped*	*2*
100 g	*mushrooms, sliced*	*4 oz*
25 g	*cornflour*	*1 oz*
450 ml	*chicken stock*	*¾ pint*
	salt and pepper	
1 tbsp	*soy sauce*	*1 tbsp*
225 g	*cooked chicken*	*8 oz*

Combine margarine and onion, cover and cook for 3 [2] minutes on high. Add the peppers, celery and mushrooms; cook for 60 [40] seconds on high. Stir in the cornflour, blend in the stock, seasoning and soy sauce. Cook on high for 5-6 [3½-4] minutes, stirring twice during cooking. Cut the chicken into bite-sized pieces and add it to the sauce. Heat on high for 2 [1½] minutes and serve hot with ribbon noodles.
For 2 servings: Cook onion 2 [1½] minutes, vegetables for 40 [30] seconds, sauce 3 [2] minutes and finally heat for 80 [60] seconds.

Timings given are for 650 [750-800] watt ovens

Chicken Chow Mein page 40

Gala Ham with Chicken

Cooking time 16 [11] minutes Serves 4

1	*onion, sliced*	*1*
3 tbsp	*demerara sugar*	*3 tbsp*
3 tbsp	*red wine vinegar*	*3 tbsp*
75 g	*celery, sliced*	*3 oz*
225 g	*gammon steak, cubed*	*8 oz*
225 g	*boned chicken, cubed*	*8 oz*
50 g	*mushrooms, sliced*	*2 oz*
3 tbsp	*redcurrant jelly*	*3 tbsp*
250 ml	*red wine*	*8 fl oz*
1 tbsp	*arrowroot*	*1 tbsp*
1 tbsp	*water*	*1 tbsp*

Combine the onion, sugar, celery and wine vinegar, cover and cook on high for 3 [2] minutes. Add the gammon and chicken, cover and cook on high for 6 [4] minutes. Stir well.

Stir the mushrooms, redcurrant jelly and wine into the meat. Cover and cook on high for 7 [5] minutes. Blend the water into the arrowroot until smooth and stir into mixture. Cover and stand for 5 minutes before serving with cooked rice or ribbon noodles. **For 2 servings:** Cook onion 2 [1½] minutes then follow with 4 [2½] minutes both times.

Chicken Rolls

Cooking time 7½-8 [5-6] minutes Serves 4

2 (225 g)	*chicken breast fillets*	*2 (8 oz)*
1	*ripe banana*	*1*
75 g	*fresh brown breadcrumbs*	*3 oz*
50 g	*ready to eat dried apricots, finely chopped*	*2 oz*
40 g	*flaked almonds*	*1½ oz*
	grated rind and juice one orange	
1	*small onion, finely chopped*	*1*
	salt and pepper	
4½ tbsp	*chicken stock or white wine*	*4½ tbsp*
25 g	*butter*	*1 oz*
	paprika	
1 tbsp	*double cream*	*1 tbsp*

Lay chicken fillets in a large polythene bag and flatten with a rolling pin or mallet. Cut each piece into 2 (four pieces in all). Mash banana and mix with breadcrumbs, apricots, orange rind and juice, onion, salt and pepper.

Season the 4 pieces of chicken and spread with stuffing. Roll up and secure with cocktail sticks and lay in a shallow dish. Melt butter on high for 40 [30] seconds and brush over chicken, sprinkle with paprika. Spoon over chicken stock or wine, cover and cook for 6-7 [4-5] minutes. Stand 5 minutes. Serve each roll sliced on individual plates.

Stir cream in remaining juices and reheat on high for 30 [20] seconds, stir and spoon over sliced chicken.
For 2 servings: Cook for 4½ [3] minutes.

Microtip

Rearrange irregular shaped items of food during cooking to ensure that the pieces cook evenly.

Timings given are for 650 [750-800] watt ovens

Chicken Breasts in Brandy and Cream Sauce

Cooking Time 23 [16] minutes Serves 4

25 g	butter	1 oz
1	medium onion, chopped	1
450 g approx	4 boneless chicken breasts	1 lb approx
2	cooking apples, peeled, cored and thickly sliced	2
2 tbsp	brandy	2 tbsp
150 ml	single cream	¼ pint
	salt and pepper	

Combine butter and onion in a shallow casserole, cover and cook on high for 3 [2] minutes.

Lay chicken breasts in onion and scatter around the apple wedges. Pour over the brandy and cream, salt and pepper. Cover and cook on high for 20 [14]* minutes. Stand for 5 minutes. Remove chicken breasts to a serving plate. Puree the apple, onion and juices to a smooth sauce. Pour a little sauce over the chicken, sprinkle with a little chopped parsley, serve remaining sauce in a jug.

This dish has a refreshing sauce despite its rich sound and is very easy to cook ahead. It can be reheated with a generous coating of sauce in a covered, shallow dish on high for 4-5 [3] minutes. Stand for 3 minutes before serving.

Serve with colourful vegetables.

Variation: This recipe is excellent with pheasant joints as an alternative to chicken.

For 2 servings: Cook onion for 2 [1½] minutes and whole dish for 14 [10] minutes.

* For 800 watt ovens cook for 12 minutes.

Chicken in Tarragon Sauce

Cooking time 28 [20] minutes Serves4

25 g	margarine	1 oz
25 g	plain flour	1 oz
150 ml	white wine	¼ pint
150 ml	water	¼ pint
4 tbsp	cream	4 tbsp
2 tsp	tarragon	2 tsp
	salt and pepper	
4 (1 kg)	chicken joints	4 (2 lb)
25 g	butter	1 oz

Melt the margarine on high for 30 [20] seconds. Stir in the flour and cook for 1 minute on high. Blend in the wine and water and cook on high for 4-5 [3½] minutes until thickened, stirring twice during cooking. Stir in the cream and tarragon. Season to taste and pour the mixture over the chicken and arrange in a casserole dish. Cover and cook on high for 22 [14-15] minutes, turn or rearrange joints halfway through cooking. Stand for 5 minutes before serving.

For 2 servings: Cook sauce 2-3 [1½-2] minutes, then complete dish 14 [10] minutes.

Easy

Chicken Kebabs

Cooking Time 5-7 [4-5] Minutes Serves 4

450 g	*boned chicken breast meat*	*1 lb*
1	*red or yellow pepper*	*1*
1	*green pepper*	*1*
100 g	*button mushrooms*	*4 oz*
	pineapple chunks	
2-4	*tomatoes — cut in quarters*	*2-4*
	bay leaves	
	orange juice	
	pepper	

Cut chicken into large chunks. De-seed and cut the peppers into pieces.

Thread the chicken, peppers, mushrooms, pineapple chunks, tomatoes and bay leaves alternatively onto wooden skewers.

Brush with fruit juice and sprinkle with pepper. Lay on plain kitchen paper and cook on high for 5-7 [4-5] minutes.

N.B. As an alternative lean pork can be used or white fish.

For 2 servings: Cook for 4 [3] minutes.

Chicken with Mustard and Lemon Sauce

Cooking time 10½ [7] minutes Serves 4

4 (100 g)	*boned chicken breasts, skinned*	*4 (1 lb)*
4 level tsp	*made wholegrain mustard*	*4 level tsp*
2 tbsp	*lemon juice*	*2 tbsp*
6 tbsp	*single cream*	*6 tbsp*

Coat the chicken breasts with the mustard and lay in a shallow dish. Sprinkle with the lemon juice. Cover and cook on high for 9 [5-6] minutes. Lift chicken onto serving dish and stir cream into juices. Cook uncovered on high for 1½ [1] minutes.

Pour sauce over chicken to serve and garnish with lemon slices and parsley. Serve with broccoli and baked potatoes.

For 2 servings: Cook for 6 [4] minutes and sauce for 60 [40] seconds.

Easy

Chicken Risotto

Cooking time 21 [14½] minutes Serves 6

50 g	*butter*	*2 oz*
1	*large onion, peeled and finely chopped*	*1*
¼	*green pepper, cored, deseeded and finely sliced*	*¼*
¼	*red pepper, cored, deseeded and finely sliced*	*¼*
2 tbsp	*tomato puree*	*2 tbsp*
1	*garlic clove, peeled and crushed*	*1*
½ tsp	*dried oregano*	*½ tsp*
50 g	*mushrooms, finely sliced*	*2 oz*
50 g	*rindless streaky bacon finely chopped*	*2 oz*
400 g	*easy-cook long-grain rice*	*14 oz*
750 ml	*hot chicken stock*	*1¼ pints*
100 g	*boneless cooked chicken finely chopped*	*4 oz*
	salt and freshly ground black pepper	
	chopped, fresh parsley to garnish	

Place the butter, onion, peppers, tomato puree, garlic, oregano, mushrooms and bacon in a large bowl, cover and cook for 8 [5½] minutes stirring half way through. Stir in the rice, stock, chicken, salt and pepper. Cover and cook for 13 [8-9] minutes. Stir half-way through cooking. Leave to stand for 5 minutes, covered. Stir with a fork, then sprinkle with chopped parsley to serve.

For 2 servings: Cook onions 6 [4] minutes then complete dish for 9 [6] minutes.

Timings given are for 650 [750-800] watt ovens

Chicken Kebabs page 44

Easy

Turkey Curry

Cooking time 15 [10½] minutes Serves 4

50 g	butter	2 oz
2 level tbsp	hot curry powder	2 level tbsp
2	medium onions, chopped	2
2	cloves of garlic, crushed	2
675 g	cooked turkey meat	1½ lb
450 ml	turkey stock	¾ pint
1 tbsp	tomato puree	1 tbsp
1 tbsp	sugar	1 tbsp
1 tbsp	lemon juice	1 tbsp
	salt and pepper	
¼ tsp	dried thyme	¼ tsp
2	bay leaves	2

Melt butter on high for 60 seconds, stir in curry powder, garlic, cover and cook on high for 4 [2½] minutes. Stir well. Stir in remaining ingredients and mix well. Cover and cook on high for 10 [7] minutes, stirring halfway through cooking. Leave to stand for 5-10 minutes, remove bay leaves and serve with cooked rice.

A tasty, useful way of using left over turkey, with the minimum of washing up — 1 serving dish.

Chicken Cacciatore

Cooking time 27 [18] minutes Serves 4

4 (approx 1 kg)	chicken joints	4 (approx 2 lbs)
225 g	mushrooms, sliced	8 oz
2 tbsp	oil	2 tbsp
1	medium onion, chopped	1
1-2	cloves garlic, crushed	1-2
2 levels tbsp	flour	2 level tbsp
150 ml	dry white wine or stock	¼ pint
1	bay leaf	1
1 tbsp	wine vinegar	1 tbsp
2 tsp	tomato puree	2 tsp
	pinch of sugar	
	salt and pepper	

Lay chicken joints in a suitable casserole dish and sprinkle over the sliced mushrooms.

Combine oil, onion and garlic in a separate bowl, cover and cook on high for 3 [2] minutes. Stir in flour then blend in wine or stock. Add remaining ingredients, cover and cook on high for 3 [2] minutes, stir well and pour over chicken and mushrooms. Cover dish and cook on high for 12 [8]* minutes, turn chicken joints over and re-arrange, cover and continue to cook for a further 12 [8]* minutes. Stand for 5 minutes before serving with cooked rice or noodles.

For 2 servings: Cook sauce for 2 [1½] minutes each time and whole dish 8 [5½] minutes both times.

* For 800 watt ovens cook for 7 minutes on high.

Microtip

A pastry flan case can be cooked quickly in the microwave; line it with absorbent kitchen paper and weigh down with ceramic cooking beans (or uncooked macaroni), cook for 4 [3] minutes on high. Remove the beans and paper, then cook for a further 60-90 [40-50] seconds until cooked.

Timings given are for 650 [750-800] watt ovens

Easy

Creamed Chicken

Cooking time 24 [16] minutes Serves 4

4 (approx 1 kg)	chicken joints	4 (approx 2 lb)
1 (290 g) can	condensed mushroom soup	1 (10½ oz) can
250 ml	single cream	8 fl oz
2	cloves garlic	2
	salt and pepper	
	paprika	

Arrange the chicken joints, skin-side down, in a casserole. Blend together the soup, cream, garlic, salt and pepper and pour over the chicken. Cover and cook on high for 12 [8]* minutes. Turn the chicken joints over. Cover, and cook for a further 12 [8]* minutes on high. Stand for 5 minutes. Sprinkle with paprika, and serve.
For 2 servings: Cook for 8 [5½] minutes.
* For 800 watt ovens cook for 7 minutes on high.

Turkey au Gratin

Easy

Cooking time 11-12 [8½] minutes Serves 4

350 g	cooked turkey meat, chopped	12 oz
2	cooking apples, peeled, cored and sliced	2
75 g	butter	3 oz
100 g	grated cheese	4 oz
300 ml	Basic White Sauce (page 69)	½ pint
4 tbsp	toasted breadcrumbs	4 tbsp

Arrange the turkey in a casserole. In a separate dish, melt the butter on high for 60 [40] seconds. Stir in the apple slices and cook on high for 2 [1½] minutes. Arrange the apple slices over the meat. Combine 75 g/3 oz of the cheese with the sauce, season to taste and pour over the apples. Sprinkle with the remaining cheese and the breadcrumbs. Cook on high for 8-9 [6] minutes. Serve hot.
For 2 servings: Cook apple for 90 [60] seconds then cook finished dish for 6 [4] minutes.

Easy

Mild Chicken Curry

Cooking time 14½ [10-10½] Serves 4

25 g	butter	1 oz
1	large onion, chopped	1
100 g	mushrooms, sliced	4 oz
1	small cooking apple, peeled, cored and chopped	1
1 tsp	curry powder	1 tsp
1 tbsp	flour	1 tbsp
300 ml	chicken stock	½ pint
275 g	cooked chicken	10 oz
150 ml	single cream	¼ pint
	salt and pepper	

Cook onion and butter together in a covered dish on high for 3 [2] minutes.

Add mushrooms and apple and cook for 1½ [1] minutes. Stir in curry powder and flour and mix well, blend in the chicken stock and cook uncovered for 5 [3½-4] minutes, stirring halfway, until sauce has thickened.

Add chicken and seasoning and cook on high for 3 [2] minutes, stir in cream and heat for 2[1½] minutes. Serve hot in a ring of boiled rice, sprinkled with a little chopped parsley for garnish.
For 2 servings: Cook onions for 2 [1½] minutes, then sauce for 3½ [2½] minutes. Add chicken and seasoning and cook for 2 [1½] minutes and 90 [60] seconds.

Duck a la Tangy Orange page 49

Chicken or Turkey Charlotte

Cooking time 26½-27½ [19-20] minutes Serves 4

100 g	butter	4 oz
1	large onion, chopped	1
40 g	plain flour	1½ oz
	salt and pepper	
300 ml	hot chicken stock	½ pint
300 ml	milk	½ pint
225 g	frozen mixed vegetables	8 oz
350 g	cooked chicken or turkey, cubed	12 oz
225 g	mushrooms, sliced	8 oz
1	clove garlic	1
225 g	toasted breadcrumbs	8 oz
4 tbsp	chopped mixed fresh herbs	4 tbsp
	tomato slices to garnish	

Place a third of the butter in a bowl with the onion and cook on high for 5 [3½] minutes. Stir in the flour and seasoning, gradually blend in the stock and milk. Cook on high for 8 [5½] minutes, stirring twice during the cooking. Stir in the vegetables, chicken or turkey and mushrooms and cook for a further 10 [7] minutes on high, stirring halfway through the cooking. In a separate bowl, melt the remaining two-thirds of butter together with the garlic on high for 1½ minutes. Stir in the breadcrumbs and mix well. Stir in the fresh herbs.

Assemble the charlotte in a glass souffle dish. Pour one third of the sauce mixture into the bottom and sprinkle over a third of the breadcrumbs. Repeat the layers, ending with a layer of crumbs. Reheat for 2-3 [1½-2] minutes on high. Garnish with tomato slices and serve.

Duck a la Tangy Orange

Cooking time 42-53 [29½-38] minutes Serves 4

1 (2 kg)	duck	1 (4-5 lb)
3 tbsp	chunky marmalade	3 tbsp
6 tbsp	dry white wine	6 tbsp
1-2 tbsp	lemon juice	1-2 tbsp
6 tbsp	stock	6 tbsp
2 tsp	cornflour	2 tbsp
2 tbsp	brandy	2 tbsp
	salt and pepper	
	cress to garnish	

Place duck, breast down on a rack. Spread the duck's back with 1 tablespoon of marmalade. Cover lightly with absorbent kitchen paper and cook on medium high for 20-25 [14-18]* minutes. Turn the duck over and spread the breast with 1
tablespoon of the marmalade. Cover and cook on medium high for a further 20-25 [14-18]* minutes. Remove the duck to serving Drain off the excess fat from the juices.

Combine the remaining marmalade, wine, lemon juice and stock. Cook on high for 2-3 [1½-2] minutes, stirring twice during cooking. Add the brandy, stir and adjust the seasoning. Serve this sauce in a jug as an accompaniment to the duck. Garnish the duck with cress to serve.

* For 800 watt ovens cook for 13 minutes on medium high.

Microtip

Cheese stored in the refrigerator can be brought to room temperature in the microwave. Remove any foil wrapping and microwave for 60-90 [40-60] seconds on low power.

Timings given are for 650 [750-800] watt ovens

VEGETABLES

Fresh vegetables are superb when cooked in a microwave oven. They require very little water (2-3 tablespoons water per 450 g/1 lb vegetables) so they retain more nutrients and have better flavour, colour and texture than if they were conventionally cooked. Frozen vegetables may be cooked from their frozen state and most require no extra water at all. Vegetables can be cooked in covered dishes in which they may be served or roasting bags, both of which save washing saucepans.

It is best to trim vegetables to a uniform size for even cooking. The larger the quantity that is cooked, the greater the time required. It is very important to allow vegetables to stand for 2-3 minutes before testing as, like other foods, they continue to cook after the oven has switched off. If after testing they are not done to your liking, then give them a little extra time.

Do not sprinkle salt on vegetables before cooking as it has a toughening effect and discolours the vegetables. You can add the salt to the water then place the vegetables in the water or add salt to taste after cooking. If you are cooking vegetables whole (such as potatoes or tomatoes) you need to prick or slice the skins to prevent them bursting. Dried vegetables can be microwaved but need to be soaked beforehand for 12 hours or overnight.

VEGETABLES

Baked potatoes cook in only a few minutes in a microwave oven. Here is a general guideline to times:
1 potato (100-150 g/4-5 oz) — 4-5 [3-4] minutes
2 potatoes — 6 [4-5] minutes
3 potatoes — 8 [6] minutes
4 potatoes — 10 [7] minutes

FRESH VEGETABLES

Vegetable	*Time on High*	*Special Notes*
Asparagus (350g/12oz)	*5-7 [4-5] minutes*	*Remove woody part. Lay in dish with stalks towards the outside of the dish. Dot with butter. Stand 3 minutes*
Broad Beans (450g/1lb)	*7-8 [5-6] minutes*	*Shell. Cook with 3-4 tablespoons water.Stir after 4 minutes. Stand 3 minutes*
Green Beans (450 g/1lb)	*12-16 [2-12] minutes*	*String and slice. Cook with 3-4 tablespoons water. Shake or stir during cooking time. Stand 3 minutes*
Broccoli or Calabrese (450g/1lb)	*8-12 [6-8] minutes*	*Trim and cut ends off stalks. Lay in dish with stalks towards the outside of the dish. Time will vary according to thickness of the stems. Stand 3 minutes*
Brussel Sprouts (450g/1lb)	*8-10 [6-7] minutes*	*Remove outer leaves and pierce or cut stalk ends. Cook with 4-5 tablespoons water. Stir or shake during cooking. Stand 3 minutes*
Cabbage (450g/1lb)	*9-12 [7-8] minutes*	*Trim and shred. Cook with 4-5 tablespoons water. Stir or shake 3 times during cooking. Stand 3 minutes*
Carrots, small (450g/1lb)	*10-12 [7-8] minutes*	*Scrape and leave whole. Stir or shake during cooking. Stand 3 minutes*
Carrots, large (450g/1lb)	*10-12 [7-8] minutes*	*Scrape and slice. Stir or shake during cooking. Stand 3 minutes*
Cauliflower (450g/1lb)	*10-12 [7-8] minutes*	*Trim and break into florets. Shake during cooking. Stand 3 minutes*
Corn-on-the-cob (2 ears)	*6-8 [4-6] minutes*	*Remove husks. Do not add water, just a knob of butter. Turn after 4 minutes. Stand 3 minutes*
Courgettes per 450 g/1 lb	*12-14 [8-10] minutes*	*Trim and slice, sprinkle with pepper and dot with butter. Do not add water. Stir or shake during cooking. Stand 2 minutes*
Leeks per 450 g/1 lb	*8-12 [6-8] minutes*	*Trim and slice. Stir or shake during cooking.*
Mange Tout per 450 g/1 lb	*4 [2½] minutes*	*Trim ends. Add knob of butter. Do not add water. Stand 2 minutes*
Mushrooms per 450 g/1 lb	*6 [4] minutes*	*Trim stalks and wipe. Do not add water, just a knob of butter. Stand 2 minutes*
Parsnips per 450 g/1 lb	*10-12 [7-8] minutes*	*Peel and slice thinly. Stir or shake during cooking. Stand 3 minutes*
Peas per 450 g/1 lb	*5-8 [4-6] minutes*	*Shell. Cooking time varies according to age. Shake during cooking. Stand 2 minutes*
Potatoes — New per 450 g/1 lb	*6-8 [4-6] minutes*	*Wash and scrub. Shake or stir during cooking. Stand 5 minutes*

VEGETABLES

Vegetable	Time on High	Special Notes
Potatoes — New per 450 g/1 lb	6-8 [4-6] minutes	Wash and scrub. Shake or stir during cooking. Stand 5 minutes
Potatoes — Old per 450 g/1 lb	8-9 [6-7] minutes	Peel and cut in chunks. Shake or stir during cooking. Stand 5 minutes
Spinach per 450 g/1 lb	6-7 [4-5] minutes	Wash and discard wilted leaves. Do not add water. Stand 3 minutes
Swede per 450 g/1 lb	18 [12] minutes	Cut into small cubes. Cook with 150 ml/¼ pint water. Stand 5 minutes

FROZEN VEGETABLES

Vegetable	Time on High	Special Notes
Asparagus per 225 g/8 oz	6-7 [4-5] minutes	Place in a shallow dish — add 2 tablespoons water, cover. Stand 3 minutes.
Beans, broad per 450 g/1 lb	7-8 [5-6] minutes	As above, with 2 tablespoons water. Stand 3 minutes.
Beans, french per 450 g/1 lb	6-7 [4-5] minutes	As above, with 3 tablespoons water. Stand 2 minutes.
Beans, runner per 450 g/1 lb	5-6 [4-5] minutes	As above, with 3 tablespoons water. Stand 2 minutes.
Broccoli per 225 g/8 oz	6-7 [4-5] minutes	Place in a shallow dish and cover. Stand 2 minutes.
Brussel Sprouts per 225 g/8 oz	7-8 [5-6] minutes	Place in a dish with 4 tablespoons water. Cover. Stand 2 minutes.
Cauliflower Florets per 225 g/8 oz	7 [4-5] minutes	Place in a dish with 2 tablespoons water. Cover, stand for 2 minutes.
Carrots per 225 g/8 oz	6-7 [4-5] minutes	Place in a shallow dish with 2 tablespoons water. Cover, stand 3 minutes.
Corn-on-the-Cob per 2 ears	6-7 [4-5] minutes	Lay in shallow dish, dot with butter, cover. Stand 2 minutes.
Courgettes per 225 g/8 oz	4-5 [3-4] minutes	Place in a shallow dish, cover. Stand 2 minutes.
Leaf Spinach per 225 g/8 oz	5-6 [4-5] minutes	As above
Mange tout per 225 g/8 oz	4-5 [3-4] minutes	As above
Mixed Vegetables per 225 g/8 oz	5-6 [4-5] minutes	Cook in covered dish or slit pouch and cook. Stand 2 minutes.
Onions, sliced per 225 g/8 oz	3-4 [2-3] minutes	Cook in covered dish. Stand 3 minutes
Peas per 225 g/2 oz	3-4 [2-3] minutes	Cook in covered dish or slit pouch and cook. Stand 2 minutes.
Sweetcorn per 225 g/8 oz	4-5 [3-4] minutes	As above

For those ovens with 'weight cook', you just programme the weight of the vegetables, select 'more' or 'less' option if required and press 'start'. The oven works out the cooking time for you.

Golden Potatoes page 54

Easy

Golden Potatoes

Cooking time 17½-20 [12-13] minutes

450 g	potatoes, peeled and cut into cubes	1 lb
3 tbsp	water	3 tbsp
1	onion, chopped	1
25 g	butter or margarine	1 oz
1 rounded tsp	turmeric	1 rounded tsp
1 tbsp	sesame seeds	1 tbsp

Place potatoes and water in a covered dish and cook on high for 10-12 [7-8] minutes.

Combine remaining ingredients together in a covered dish and cook on high for 6 [4] minutes.

Drain potatoes and toss in the turmeric mixture, reheat 1½-2 [1] minutes to serve.

This dish can be prepared ahead and reheated, covered on high for 5-6 [4] minutes.

For 2 servings: Cook potatoes for 7[5] minutes, turmeric mixture for 4[2½] minutes and reheat for 90[60] seconds.

Easy

Creamed Potatoes

Cooking Time 17 [12] minutes Serves 4

800 g	potatoes — peeled and cut in chunks	1 lb 12 oz
6 tbsp	milk	4 fl oz
25 g	butter	1 oz
	salt and pepper	

Combine potatoes, milk and butter in a deep casserole to allow for milk boiling up. Cover and cook on high for 17 [12] minutes until soft. Leave to stand 5 minutes. Do not drain but mash the potatoes into the milky juices. Season to taste and serve hot.

For 2 servings: Cook potatoes for 12 [8] minutes.

Scalloped Potatoes

Cooking time 24 [18] minutes Serves 4-6

4	large potatoes, peeled and thinly sliced	4
	salt and pepper	
2 tsp	mustard powder	2 tsp
50 g	grated cheese	2 oz
2 tbsp	flour	2 tbsp
2	onions, thinly sliced	2
50 g	margarine, cut into pieces	2 oz
300 ml	milk	½ pint
	paprika	

Rinse and dry the potato slices. Grease a suitable dish and lay a third of potato slices in it. Mix salt, pepper, mustard powder, cheese and flour together. Scatter half the onions over the potatoes then sprinkle them with a third of the cheese mixture. Repeat the layers, ending with the cheese mixture. Dot with margarine and pour the milk over the potatoes. Sprinkle with paprika. Cover and cook on high for 24 [18] minutes. Stand for 5 minutes before serving.

For 2 servings: Cook for 16 [12] minutes.

Microtip

Both density and size influence microwave cooking time. To cook different vegetables together, they should be cut into different sizes to give even results. For example, large florets of cauliflower, fairly thin slices of carrot, whole sprouts (with a cross cut in the base) and potatoes shaped into small balls can all be cooked together with even results. Remember to stand for 3 minutes before testing.

Timings given are for 650 [750-800] watt ovens

Creamed Leeks

Cooking time 21 [16] minutes Serves 4

575 g	Potatoes, peeled and cut in small chunks	1 lb 4 oz
225 g	leeks, washed and sliced	8 oz
5 tbsp	water	5 tbsp
25 g	margarine	1 oz
	salt and pepper	
50 g	full fat cream cheese	2 oz
50 g	grated cheddar cheese	2 oz
1 tbsp	toasted breadcrumbs	1 tbsp

Combine potatoes, leeks and water in covered casserole dish and cook on high for 16 [12] minutes. Stand 5 minutes before testing if cooked — leeks and potatoes should be soft enough to mash.

Drain and mash with margarine. Add salt and pepper to taste and finally blend in the cream cheese. Smooth the surface or turn into a shallow dish.

Combine grated cheese and toasted breadcrumbs and sprinkle over the surface. Cook uncovered on high for 5 [4] minutes. Serve hot.

This dish is so versatile, it is delicious served with baked ham, gammon steaks, grilled bacon or sausages. It is also equally good with grilled meats. It will freeze very successfully at the stage before adding cheese. When thawed, sprinkle over the grated cheese and breadcrumbs and reheat on high for 7 [5] minutes.

For 2 servings: Cook for 10-11 [8] minutes. With cheese topping cook for 3 [2] minutes.

Easy

Garlic Green Beans

Cooking time 10-11 [7½-8½] minutes Serves 4

450 g	frozen green beans	1 lb
40 g	butter	1½ oz
1-2 tbsp	salad oil	1-2 tbsp
2 tsp	chopped parsley	2 tsp
1	clove garlic, crushed	1
	salt and pepper	

Cook the beans in 2 tablespoons of water in a covered dish for 6-7 [4-5] minutes on high. Drain them. In a separate bowl, melt the butter on high for 60 [40] seconds. Add the oil, parsley and garlic. Cook for 60 [40] seconds. Add the beans, salt and pepper. Toss well, cover and cook on high for 2 [1½] minutes.

Variation: Cook 2 rashers of rindless steaky bacon until crisp and crumble them over the beans just before serving.

For 2 servings: Cook beans for 4-5 [3-4] minutes. Cook dessing for 40 [30] seconds each time and finally reheat for 90 [60] seconds.

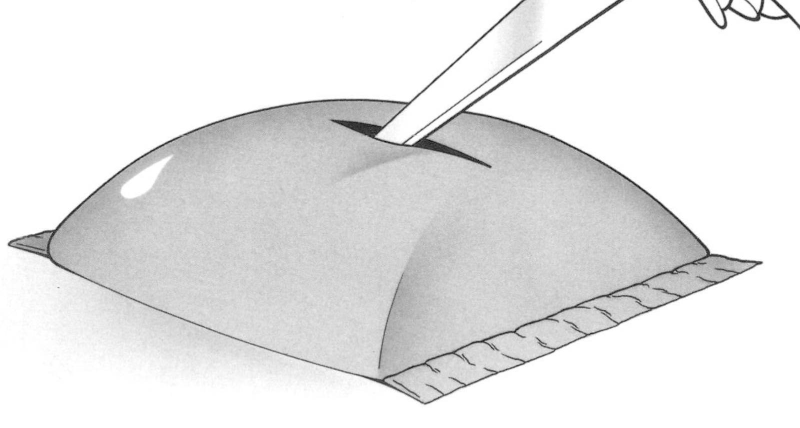

Microtip

Commercially, frozen vegetables or boil-in-the-bag dishes can be cooked in the bags in the microwave. Make sure the bag is slit with a knife to prevent ballooning.

Timings given are for 650 [750-800] watt ovens

Herby Tomatoes page 57
Stir-Fry Courgettes and Mushrooms page 59

Easy

Herby Tomatoes

Cooking time 4-5 [2-3] minutes Serves 4

4	*tomatoes*	*4*
25 g	*butter or margarine, cut into pieces*	*1 oz*
3-4	*spring onions, sliced*	*3-4*
2 tbsp	*fresh chopped parsley*	*2 tbsp*
1	*clove garlic, crushed (optional)*	*1*
½ tsp	*dried tarragon*	*½ tsp*
1 tsp	*dried oregano*	*1 tsp*
	salt and pepper	

Cut the tomatoes in half and arrange them in a shallow dish, cut side uppermost. Dot them with butter and sprinkle them with the remaining ingredients. Cover the tomatoes and cook on high for 4-5 [2-3] minutes, depending on the ripeness of the tomatoes.

N.B. These are ideal to serve with grilled meats or as a tasty snack with toast or crispy bread.

For 2 servings: Cook for 2½-3 [2] minutes.

Easy

Honey Glazed Carrots

Cooking time 11 [8] minutes Serves 4

450 g	*young carrots, scrubbed*	*1 lb*
25 g	*butter*	*1 oz*
1 tbsp	*honey*	*1 tbsp*
	generous pinch ground cinnamon	

If the carrots are small, leave them whole. Cut larger ones in half. Cook the carrots in 3 tablespoons water in a covered dish on high for 10 [7] minutes. Drain them. Melt the butter and honey on high for 60 [40] seconds and pour this over the carrots. Toss well, sprinkle with cinnamon and serve.

For 2 servings: Cook carrots for 7 [5] and glaze for 40 [30] seconds.

Vegetable Bake

Cooking time 22 [16½] minutes Serves 4

1	*onion, chopped*	*1*
25 g	*margarine*	*1 oz*
25 g	*plain flour*	*1 oz*
300 ml	*milk*	*½ pint*
	salt and pepper	
	pinch nutmeg	
3 tbsp	*single cream*	*3 tbsp*
350 g	*potatoes, peeled, sliced*	*12 oz*
75 g	*mushrooms, sliced*	*3 oz*
1	*stick celery, chopped*	*1*
50 g	*grated cheese*	*2 oz*
25 g	*toasted breadcrumbs*	*1 oz*

Rinse potato slices in cold water to remove starch and leave to drain. Combine onion and margarine, cover and cook on high for 3 [2] minutes. Stir in flour, blend in the milk gradually. Cook uncovered, on high for 3 [2½] minutes. Stir well until thickened.

Stir in seasoning, nutmeg, cream, potatoes, mushrooms and celery. Turn into an oven proof dish, sprinkle with grated cheese and breadcrumbs. Cook uncovered on high for 16 [12] minutes. Leave to stand for 5 minutes.

For 2 servings: Cook onion for 2 [1½] minutes and sauce for 2 [1½] minutes. Cook whole dish for 11 [8] minutes.

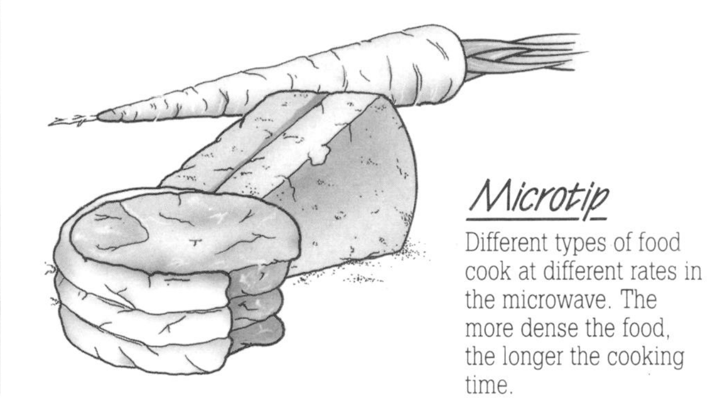

Microtip

Different types of food cook at different rates in the microwave. The more dense the food, the longer the cooking time.

Timings given are for 650 [750-800] watt ovens

Easy

Cauliflower with crunchy topping

Cooking time 8-9 [6-7] minutes Serves 4

1	*cauliflower broken into florets*	*1*
75 g	*butter*	*3 oz*
50 g	*toasted breadcrumbs*	*2 oz*
2 tbsp	*finely chopped fresh parsley*	*2 tbsp*
1 tbsp	*lemon juice*	*1 tbsp*

Cook the cauliflower florets in a covered dish with 3 tablespoons water on high for 6-7 [4-5] minutes. Drain them. Melt the butter on high for 60 [40] seconds and stir in the remaining ingredients. Cook for a further 60 [40] seconds on high. Spoon the topping over the cauliflower and serve hot.
N.B. This crunchy topping can be used to spoon over cooked broccoli.
For 2 servings: Cook cauliflower for 4-5 [3-4] minutes. Melt butter and cook topping for 40 [30] seconds each time.

Easy

Celery au Gratin

Cooking time 17 [12] minutes Serves 4

1	*head of celery, cut in 10 cm/4 in lengths*	*1*
150 ml	*boiling stock*	*¼ pint*
100g	*grated cheese*	*4 oz*
4 tbsp	*toasted breadcrumbs*	*4 tbsp*
50 g	*butter*	*2 oz*

Cook the celery in the stock in a covered dish for 14 [10] minutes on high. Drain the celery. Sprinkle it with the cheese and breadcrumbs. Dot with the butter and cook, uncovered, for 3 [2] minutes on high.
For 2 servings: Cook celery for 9 [6-7] minutes. Finally cook for 2 [1½] minutes.

Courgettes and Sweetcorn Gratin

Cooking time 21 [16] minutes Serves 4

450 g	*courgettes, sliced*	*1 lb*
2-3	*spring onions, sliced*	*2-3*
	black pepper	
1 tbsp	*lemon juice*	*1 tbsp*
40 g	*butter*	*1½ oz*
100 g	*frozen sweetcorn, thawed*	*4 oz*
25 g	*flour*	*1 oz*
300 ml	*milk*	*½ pint*
100 g	*grated cheese*	*4 oz*
25 g	*toasted breadcrumbs*	*1 oz*

Arrange courgettes evenly in the base of a shallow ovenproof dish. Sprinkle over spring onions, pepper, lemon juice and dot with 15 g (1½ oz) butter. Cover and cook on high for 10 [7] minutes.

In a separate bowl melt the remaining butter on high for 50 [40] seconds. Stir in the flour and cook for 50 [40] seconds. Blend in the milk and cook uncovered on high for 3 [2] minutes, stirring halfway through cooking. Beat well until it thickens, stir in 75 g (3 oz) of the cheese, the juices from the courgettes and the sweetcorn. Heat through on high for 2 minutes and pour over courgettes. Scatter over remaining cheese and toasted breadcrumbs and cook uncovered on high for 4 [3] minutes.
For 2 servings: Cook courgettes for 7 [5] minutes. For sauce cook 30 seconds and 2 [1½] minutes. Heat through for 60-90 seconds and finally for 2½ [2] minutes.

Timings given are for 650 [750-800] watt ovens

Easy

Onions with Apples

Cooking time 10 [11] minutes

450 g	*onions, sliced*	*1 lb*
3	*cooking apples, approx 12 oz peeled, cored and sliced*	*3*
3 tbsp	*cooking oil*	*3 tbsp*
1 tsp	*curry powder*	*1 tsp*
	salt	
2 tbsp	*cream*	*2 tbsp*

Combine all ingredients, except cream, and cook in a covered dish on high for 8 [5½] minutes. Continue to cook on medium power for 6 [4] minutes. Stir in the cream and heat a further 2 [1½] minutes on medium. Serve with grilled or roast meats. This dish can be frozen for up to 3 months.
For 2 servings: Cook for 5 [3½] minutes on high. Followed by 4 [3] minutes on medium power and heat through a further 90 [60] seconds on medium power.

Stir-Fry Courgettes and Mushrooms

Cooking Time 7-8 [5½-6] minutes

225 g	*courgettes*	*8 oz*
175 g	*tomatoes, skinned*	*6 oz*
75 g	*mushrooms, thinly sliced*	*3 oz*
	salt and pepper	
50 g	*derinded streaky bacon*	*2 oz*

Lay bacon rashers on a rack or plate, cover with a piece of plain kitchen paper and cook on high for 3-4 [2½-3] minutes, until crisp.

Cut courgettes into 5 cm (2") sticks or put through a chipper disc in a food processor. Halve tomatoes and remove pips, cut flesh into strips.

Combine courgettes and mushrooms in a dish and cook uncovered on high for 2½ [2] minutes. Stir well and add seasoning and tomatoes. Cook a further 1½ [1] minute. Crumble bacon or snip into small pieces and stir into vegetables to serve.
For 2 servings: Cook bacon for 2 [1½] minutes. Cook vegetables for 1½ [1] minutes followed by 60 [40] seconds.

Easy

Ratatouille

Cooking time 25 [17] minutes Serves 4-6

2	*Onions, chopped*	*2*
2	*cloves garlic, chopped*	*2*
1	*large aubergine, chopped*	*1*
1	*red pepper, deseeded and chopped*	*1*
1	*green pepper, deseeded and chopped*	*1*
225g	*courgettes, chopped*	*8 oz*
1 (400 g) can	*tomatoes, chopped*	*1 (14 oz) can*
2 tbsp	*oil*	*2 tbsp*
1 tbsp	*tomatoe puree*	*1 tbsp*
	salt and pepper	
½ tsp	*oregano*	*½ tsp*

Cook the onions and garlic in the oil on high for 3 [2] minutes until soft. Add the aubergine, peppers and courgettes, cover and cook on high for 4 [3] minutes. Add remaining ingredients and cook uncovered, for 18 [12] minutes on high. Serve hot or cold.
For 2 servings: Cook onions for 2 [1½] minutes. With aubergines, etc, cook 2½ [2] minutes. Cook finally for 12 [8] minutes.

Timings given are for 650 [750-800] watt ovens

SUPPER DISHES AND SNACKS

For snacks and supper dishes a microwave is a boon, be it for reheating convenience foods or preparing and cooking them. One of the great attractions is the ease and economy of cooking for one person a snack or light meal. Many lunch or supper dishes can be prepared ahead and just reheated when required. Cheese and eggs often form the base of these foods and because they are high in fat, which attracts the microwave, you need to take care not to overcook them.

Eggs can be cooked in most ways except boiling in the shells, which due to build-up of pressure could explode. They probably will not harm the oven but the mess they make is enough to ensure you do not make the same mistake twice! If poaching eggs in a dish or frying them in the browning dish, pierce the yolk with a knife to break the membrane. Egg yolk cooks more quickly than egg white, so you will obtain a more even result if cooking on medium power. Scrambled eggs are very suitable for microwaving since, not only do they have a light fluffy texture but they do not stick to the bowl or dish.

To obtain an attractive cheese topping in ovens without a browning facility mix equal quantities of browned breadcrumbs and grated cheese, sprinkling over the dish and cook.

SUPPER DISHES AND SNACKS

Pasta and rice need to be rehydrated so need cooking for as long as in a conventional way. The advantage is a steam free kitchen and not having the pasta or rice sticking to the base of the pan. Allow a large enough container for the water to boil up. Leave to stand for 5-10 minutes before draining.
You will find your microwave ideal for defrosting and reheating cooked rice and pasta. From frozen allow 5 minutes per 450 g/1 lb cooked rice/pasta on defrost, then reheat on high for 3-4 minutes.

PLAIN EGG DISHES

	Ingredients	***Method (per 1 portion)***
Scrambled Egg	*2 eggs 3 tablespoons milk salt and pepper knob of butter*	*Beat eggs, milk and seasoning in a jug or bowl, add butter and cook on high for 1¾-2 [1½] minutes, stirring halfway through cooking and at the end.*
Baked Egg	*1 egg salt and pepper*	*Break egg into a ramekin dish, pierce yolk with point of knife. Season, cover and cook on medium for 60-70 [40-60] seconds. Stand 1 minute*
Fried Egg	*knob of butter 1 egg salt and pepper*	*Melt butter in shallow dish or saucer on high for 20 seconds. Break in egg and pierce yolk. Season to taste, cover and cook on medium for 40-60 [30-40] seconds. Stand 1 minute.*
Poached Egg	*1 egg 1 tablespoon vinegar 6 tbsp water*	*Place water and vinegar in a ramekin or small dish, cook on high for 1½-2 [1-1½] minutes until boiling. Break in egg, pierce yolk and cook uncovered for 60 [40] seconds on medium or 40-60 [30-40] seconds on high. Stand for 1 minute. Drain off water and vinegar.*

RICE AND PASTA

	Ingredients	***Method (4 portions)***
Boiled Rice	*225g/8oz*	*Combine rice with 1 pint of cold water in a deep container. Cover and cook on high for 6 [4] minutes. Stir well and continue cooking for 15 [10] minutes on medium low. Stand for 10 minutes before serving.*
Pasta Shells/Noodles	*225g/8oz*	*Combine pasta with 900 ml/1½ pints of boiling water and one tablespoon of cooking oil in a deep container. Cover and cook on high for 14 [10] minutes. Stir well and leave to stand for 10 minutes to complete cooking before serving.*
Quick Cook Spaghetti	*225g/8oz*	*Combine spaghetti with boiling water as above for pasta and cook on high for 6 [4]. Leave to stand for 10 minutes to complete cooking, before serving.*

Bacon Gratin page 65

Ham and Asparagus Tagliatelle page 67

Easy

Cauliflower and Bacon Cheese

Cooking time 18 [14] minutes Serves 4

1	*cauliflower, broken into florets*	*1*
175 g	*rindless bacon rashers*	*6 oz*
25 g	*margarine*	*1 oz*
25 g	*plain flour*	*1 oz*
300 ml	*milk*	*½ pint*
½ tsp	*mustard powder*	*½ tsp*
	salt and pepper	
75 g	*grated cheese*	*3 oz*

Cook the cauliflower florets with 3 tablespoons of water, covered, for 5 [4] minutes on high. Drain them.

Cover the bacon with absorbent kitchen paper and cook it on a rack for 5 [4] minutes on high. Drain it on absorbent kitchen paper and chop or crumble it. Melt the margarine on high for 40 [30] seconds; stir in the flour and cook on high for 40 [30] seconds. Blend in the milk gradually. Cook on high for 4 [3] minutes, stirring twice during the cooking. Stir in salt and pepper to taste, mustard, 50 g/2 oz cheese and the bacon. Pour the mixture over the cauliflower florets. Sprinkle with the remaining cheese and cook on high for 2½ [2] minutes. Serve hot as a lunch or supper dish.

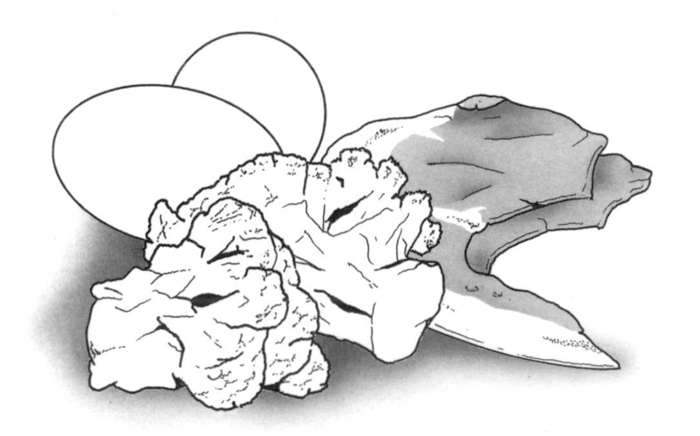

Creamed Eggs in Corn and Cheese Sauce

6	*eggs — hard boiled*	*6*
275 g can	*sweetcorn*	*10 oz can*
25 g	*butter or margarine*	*1 oz*
25 g	*flour*	*1 oz*
300 ml	*milk*	*½ pint*
4 tbsp	*single cream*	*4 tbsp*
	salt and pepper	
	good pinch nutmeg	
100 g	*grated cheese*	*4 oz*
2 tsp	*made mustard*	*2 tsp*
	Topping	
2 tbsp	*toasted breadcrumbs*	*2 tbsp*
50 g	*grated cheese*	*2 oz*

Drain liquid from sweetcorn and sprinkle over the base of a shallow dish. Cut eggs in half and lay cut side down on sweetcorn.

In a bowl or jug melt the margarine or butter on high for 60 [40] seconds, stir in flour and cook a further 60 [40] seconds. Blend in milk and cook for 3 [2] minutes on high, stirring halfway through cooking. Stir in seasoning to taste, cheese and cream. Pour sauce over eggs and sweetcorn. Combine breadcrumbs and cheese and scatter over surface. If serving straightaway heat through on high for 2-3 [1½-2] minutes. If prepared ahead and heating from cold, cook on high for 4-5 [3½-4] minutes. The top can be crispened up under a grill for a few minutes.

For 2 servings: Cook sauce for 40 [30] seconds each time followed by 2 [1½] minutes. Heat through with cheese topping for 2½-3 [2] minutes.

This makes a good tasty dish which can be served with crispy bread or a green salad.

Easy

Bacon Gratin

Cooking time 8 [6] minutes Serves 4

25 g	margarine	1 oz
100 g	onion, chopped	4 oz
1 tsp	dried parsley flakes or	1 tsp
1 tbsp	freshly chopped parsley	1 tbsp
225 g	cooked bacon joint, chopped	8 oz
1 (225 g) can	tomatoes	1 (8 oz) can
100 g	grated cheese	4 oz
50 g	toasted breadcrumbs	2 oz

Combine the margarine and onion in a pie dish and cook on high for 3 [2] minutes. Stir in parsley, bacon and the tomatoes with their juice. Season to taste and smooth the surface. Mix the grated cheese and breadcrumbs together and sprinkle over surface. Cook on high for 5 [4] minutes. Serve hot with crusty bread or baked potatoes. Stand for 3 minutes before serving.

For 2 servings: Cook onion for 2 [1½] minutes. Heat through for 3 [2] minutes.

Golden Baked Potatoes

Cooking time 16-17 [11½-12] minutes Serves 4

4	large potatoes for baking, scrubbed	4
3	rashers streaky bacon — derind	3
100 g	cream cheese	4 oz
1-2 tbsp	milk	1-2 tbsp
2 tsp	chopped parsley	2 tsp
	salt and pepper	
50 g	grated cheddar cheese	2 oz
25 g	toasted breadcrumbs	1 oz

Prick potatoes with a fork and wrap each one loosely in kitchen paper. Place on turntable and cook on high for approximately 10 [7] minutes (depending on size). Leave to stand on one side for 10 minutes to complete cooking.

Place bacon rashers on a rack or plate and cover with a piece of kitchen paper. Cook on high for 2-3 [1½-2] minutes until crisp. Leave to cool, then crumble or chop.

Cut potatoes in half and scoop out flesh into a bowl. Mash well with cream cheese. Add seasoning, parsley and bacon and enough milk to make soft mixture. Pile back into potato shells, sprinkle with grated cheese and breadcrumbs and cook on high for 4 [3] minutes to heat through. Stand for 2 minutes before serving.

Easy

Cheese and Asparagus Charlotte

Cooking time 22 [15½] minutes Serves 4

6	slices of wholemeal bread — buttered	6
275-350 g can	asparagus spears — drained	10-12 oz can
175 g	grated cheese	6 oz
3	eggs	3
600 ml	milk	1 pint
	salt and pepper	
	pinch of dried mustard	
25 g	toasted breadcrumbs	1 oz

Remove crusts from bread and cut into squares or fingers. Lay half of them butter side down in the base of an ovenproof gratin dish. Cover bread with asparagus and sprinkle with half the cheese. Cover with remaining bread. Beat eggs together with milk, seasoning and mustard and pour over bread, leave to stand 20-30 minutes. Cook uncovered on medium power for 20 [14] minutes to set custard. Combine remaining cheese with toasted breadcrumbs and cook on high for 2 [1½] minutes.

Timings given are for 650 [750-800] watt ovens

Easy

Egg and Bacon Pasta

Cooking time 8 [6] minutes Serves 2

100 g	*streaky bacon*	*4 oz*
175 g	*spaghetti cooked and drained (page 61)*	*6 oz*
2	*eggs*	*2*
2-3 tbsp	*single cream*	*2-3 tbsp*
75 g	*grated cheese*	*3 oz*
	salt and pepper	

Cook the bacon on a rack, covered with kitchen paper, on high for 5 [4] minutes, until crisp. Chop or crumble it and mix with the hot spaghetti. Beat the eggs with the cream and seasoning, add 50 g/2 oz of the cheese and stir into hot spaghetti. Cook on high for 3 [2] minutes. Stir well. Sprinkle with the remaining cheese and serve hot.

Easy

Leek and Macaroni Cheese

Cooking time 15-16 [10½-11] minutes Serves 4-6

50 g	*butter*	*2 oz*
275 g	*leeks, sliced*	*10 oz*
25 g	*flour*	*1 oz*
450 ml	*milk*	*¾pint*
175 g	*grated cheese*	*6 oz*
	salt and pepper	
100 g	*shortcut macaroni, cooked*	*4 oz*
2 tbsp	*toasted breadcrumbs*	*2 tbsp*

Melt the butter on high for 60 [40] seconds, add the leeks and cook, covered, on high for 6 [4] minutes. Stir in the flour, then gradually stir in the milk and cook on high for 5-6 [3½-4] minutes until thickened. Stir in 100 g/4 oz cheese and seasoning and macaroni. Pour into shallow dish and sprinkle with the remaining cheese and breadcrumbs. Cook on high for 3 [2] minutes. Serve hot.

For 2 servings: Cook leeks 5 [4] minutes. Cook sauce 3 [2] minutes and heat through for 2 [1½] minutes.

Easy

Creamed Pasta

Cooking time 11-13 [9-10] minutes Serves 4

225 g	*pasta shells — cooked*	*8 oz*
4-6	*rashers streaky bacon*	*4-6*
275 g can	*condensed mushroom soup*	*10½ oz can*
100 g	*frozen peas — thawed*	*4 oz*
	salt and pepper	
100 g	*grated cheese*	*4 oz*
2 tbsp	*toasted breadcrumbs*	*2 tbsp*

Cook rashers of bacon on rack, covered with kitchen paper, on high for 4-5 [3-4] minutes until crisp, chop or crumble. Combine pasta shells, bacon, condensed soup, peas and seasoning, turn into a shallow dish and sprinkle over the cheese and breadcrumbs. Cook on high for 7-8 [6] minutes uncovered. Leave to stand for 2-3 minutes before serving.

For 2 servings: Cook bacon 2-2½ [1½-2] minutes. Heat through for 3-4 [2-3] minutes.

Easy

Pasticcio

Cooking time 16-18 [12-13] minutes Serves 3-4

25 g	margarine	1 oz
1	small onion, chopped	1
225 g	lean minced beef	8 oz
225 g	tomatoes, chopped	8 oz
	salt and pepper	
$\frac{3}{4}$ tsp	nutmeg	$\frac{3}{4}$ tsp
50 g	grated cheese	2 oz
100 g	cooked short macaroni	4 oz
300 ml	Basic White Sauce (page 69)	$\frac{1}{2}$ pint
50 g	toasted breadcrumbs	2 oz

Combine margarine and onion in a dish, cover and cook on high for 3 [2] minutes. Stir in the beef and cook on high for 3 [2] minutes. Stir in tomatoes, salt and pepper and nutmeg and cook on high for 6-7 [5] minutes, uncovered until liquid is reduced. Pour into a dish. Combine 25 g/1 oz of the cheese with the macaroni and arrange the mixture over the beef. Cover with the white sauce. Mix together remaining cheese and breadcrumbs and sprinkle over sauce. Cook uncovered on high for 4-5 [3-4] minutes. Serve hot.

Bolognese Sauce Easy

Cooking time 18 [12½] minutes Serves 4

4	rashers streaky bacon, finely chopped	4
1	medium onion, finely chopped	1
1	large garlic clove, crushed	1
25 g	plain flour	1 oz
225 g	minced beef	8 oz
75 g	chicken livers, finely chopped	3 oz
1 (400 g) can	tomatoes	1 (14 oz) can
4 tbsp	tomato puree	4 tbsp
300 ml	hot beef stock	$\frac{1}{2}$ pint
100 g	mushrooms, sliced	4 oz
	salt and freshly ground black pepper	
1 tsp	dried basil	1 tsp

Place the bacon, onion and garlic in a bowl. Cover and cook on high for 5[3½] minutes, stirring halfway through. Stir in the flour, beef, chicken livers, tomatoes and tomato puree. Cover and cook on high for 3[2] minutes. Stir in stock, mushrooms, salt pepper and basil. Cover and cook on high for 10[7] minutes. Stir halfway through. Stand for 5 minutes before serving with cooked pasta, (see page 61).

Ham and Asparagus Tagliatelle

Cooking time 13½-14½ [10-11] minutes Serves 4

450 g	cooked bacon joint, chopped or minced	1 lb
275 g can	asparagus, cut pieces	10 oz can
500 ml approx	milk	1 pint approx
50 g	margarine	2 oz
50 g	flour	2 oz
	salt and pepper	
175 g	tagliatelle verdi — cooked	6 oz

Drain liquid from asparagus and make up to 750 ml (1¼ pint) with milk.

Melt margarine in a large bowl on high for 90 [60] seconds, stir in flour and cook a further 60 [40] seconds. Gradually, blend in the liquid and cook uncovered on high for 7-8 [5-6] minutes stirring halfway through cooking. Stir in seasoning, using salt sparingly as bacon will be a little salty.

In a suitable 1.5 litre (2 ¾ pint) shallow dish, sprinkle base with one third of bacon, cover with half of the pasta and pour over half the sauce. Cover sauce with another third of bacon, then the chopped asparagus, remaining pasta and the remaining bacon. Cover with remaining sauce and if serving straight away reheat uncovered on high for 4 [3] minutes. If prepared ahead and reheated from cold, cook on high for 7-8 [6] minutes. Stand for 3 minutes before serving.

Variation: use 350 g [12 oz] sweetcorn in place of asparagus and use 750 ml [1¼] pint milk for sauce.

SAUCES

Once you have mastered the techniques of sauce-making in the microwave you will never use a saucepan again. Sauces can be made so quickly and easily that you will find yourself serving them with meals more frequently than ever before. Often they can be cooked in the jugs in which they are to be served, so not only do you save on washing up burnt saucepans, but there are no cooking containers to wash at all.

For a successful, smooth sauce make sure the ingredients are blended well together before cooking, then it is usually only necessary to stir briskly halfway through cooking and again at the end. Some of the sauces for which the preparation is more critical will need stirring several times during cooking. Sauces can also be prepared in advance (a few hours beforehand or the day before) left covered to prevent a skin forming, and reheated just before serving.

Many dishes require a quantity of basic white sauce amongst the ingredients. A useful way of having a ready to use home made sauce is to make a stick of white sauce roux and store in the freezer. Soften 175 g/6 oz margarine on medium low for 60 [40] seconds and stir in 350 g/12 oz dried milk powder, 175 g/6 oz plain flour, salt and pepper and bind together with 3 tablespoons of water. Mix to smooth ball then shape into a 15 cm/6" roll in waxed paper or cooking film. Freeze for up to 3 months or store in refrigerator.

White Sauce using Roux Stick

To make sauce bring 300 ml/½ pint of water to boil in the microwave on high for 3-4 [2-3] minutes. Crumble in 2½cm/1" of roux stick stirring well until smooth. Cook for a further 1½ [1] minutes on high until thick and smooth. This roux stick makes it very easy to make small portions of sauce by reducing quantities and time accordingly.

Instant Packet Sauces

For a 300ml/½ pint sachet of instant sauce blend a little cold water with the packet contents to a smooth paste. Make up to 300 ml/½ pint with cold water and cook on high for 2½-3 [2] minutes stirring halfway, until thickened. Stand for 1-2 minutes before serving.
NB: Onion Sauce may need to be cooked an extra 1-2 minutes.

Instant Gravy

For instant gravy using granules blend 2 tablespoons of cold water with 4 tablespoons of gravy granules to a paste. Make up to 300 ml/½ pint with cold water and cook as for instant sauces, above.

Gravy *Easy*

Cooking Time 6½ [4½] Minutes
Makes about 600 ml/1 pint

	juices from meat or poultry	
25 g	*plain flour*	*1 oz*
450 ml	*vegetable stock or water*	*¾pint*
1	*stock cube*	*1*
	salt and pepper	

Drain and discard most of the fat from the juices. Transfer the juices to a bowl and stir in the flour. Cook on high for 30 [20] seconds. Blend in the stock or water and crumble a stock cube into the liquid. Cook on high for 6 [4] minutes, stirring halfway through the cooking time. Season to taste.

Basic White Sauce *Easy*

Cooking time 5 [4] Minutes
Makes about 300 ml/½ pint

25 g	*margarine or butter*	*1 oz*
25 g	*plain flour*	*1 oz*
300 ml	*milk*	*½ pint*
	salt and white pepper	

Melt the margarine or butter in a jug or bowl on high for 60 [40] seconds. Stir in the flour and cook on high for 60 [40] seconds, blend in the milk gradually, stirring well or whisking. Cook, uncovered, on high for 3 [2] minutes, stirring halfway through the cooking time and at the end. Season to taste.

To make bechamel sauce, pour milk into a jug and add a sprig of thyme, ½ small onion, a small bay leaf and ¼ teaspoon of nutmeg. Cook for 3 minutes on high. Leave to infuse for 15 minutes, strain and use as above.

Mushroom Sauce for Chicken

Cooking Time 9 [6½] Minutes
Makes about 450 ml/¾ pint

1 tbsp	*oil*	*1 tbsp*
25 g	*margarine*	*1 oz*
6	*spring onions, chopped*	*6*
100 g	*mushrooms, sliced*	*4 oz*
25 g	*plain flour*	*1 oz*
300 ml	*chicken stock*	*½ pint*
	salt and pepper	
	pinch of nutmeg	
2 tbsp	*freshly chopped parsley*	*2 tbsp*
2 tbsp	*dry white wine or sherry*	*2 tbsp*

Combine oil, margarine and spring onions. Cook on high for 2 [1½] minutes. Add the mushrooms and cook on high for 60 [40] seconds. Stir in the flour and cook on high for 60 [40] seconds. Add the stock, seasoning and parsley and stir. Cook on high for 5 [3½] minutes, stirring twice during cooking. Stir in the wine and adjust the seasoning. Serve hot with cooked chicken joints, or combine with cooked chicken flesh and serve on a bed of cooked rice.

Timings given are for 650 [750-800] watt ovens

Sweet and Sour Sauce

Cooking Time 13 [9] Minutes

Makes about 250ml/8 fl oz.

1	onion, chopped	1
1	carrot, cut into thin strips	1
½	green pepper, cut into thin strips	½
½	red pepper, cut into thin strips	½
1	clove garlic, crushed	1
2 tbsp	oil	2 tbsp
1 level tbsp	cornflour	1 level tbsp
2 tbsp	soy sauce	2 tbsp
2 tbsp	tomato ketchup	2 tbsp
2 tbsp	wine vinegar	2 tbsp
225 g can	pineapple pieces	7½-8 oz can

Combine onion, carrot, peppers and garlic with oil, cover and cook on high for 8 [5½] minutes. In a separate bowl blend soy sauce into cornflour, together with ketchup and wine vinegar. Drain juices from pineapple and add the juices to the cornflour mixture. Pour mixture into vegetables together with pinapple pieces. Cover and cook on high for 5 [3½] minutes, stir well adding 1-2 tablespoons of water if a little too thick.

This sauce is useful to combine with left over chicken flesh or freshly cooked fish.

Lean strips 4 x ½ cm (1½" x ½") of pork or chicken breast can be quickly browned in a pan and added to this sauce for a sweet and sour dish.

Easy

Apple Sauce

Cooking Time 3 [2] Minutes

Makes about 350 g/12 oz

2-3	cooking apples (about 350 g/12 oz) peeled, cored and chopped	2-3
1 tbsp	water	1 tbsp
25 g	butter	1 oz
1 tbsp	lemon juice	1 tbsp
	sugar to taste	

Combine the apples and water in a covered dish and cook on high for 3-4 [2-3] minutes. Beat until smooth and stir in the remaining ingredients. Serve with roast pork and poultry.

Hollandaise Sauce

Cooking Time 3 [2] Minutes

Makes about 250 ml/8 fl oz

100 g	butter	4 oz
	juice of 1 lemon	
2	egg yolks	2
	salt and pepper	

Melt the butter in a jug on high for 2 [1½] minutes. Add the lemon juice and egg yolks and whisk thoroughly. Cook for 30-40 [20-30] seconds on high, whisking once during the cooking and at the end. Serve with poached salmon or broccoli.

Microtip

Toasted almonds can be made in the microwave. Sprinkle 50 g/2 oz flaked almonds on the glass tray and microwave on high for 3½-4½ [2½-3] minutes, stirring halfway through cooking, then stand for 5 minutes.

Timings given are for 650 [750-800] watt ovens

Easy

Bread Sauce

Cooking Time 6-7 [5] Minutes

Makes about 300 ml/½ pint

1	onion	1
6	whole cloves	6
300 ml	milk	½ pint
50 g	fresh white breadcrumbs	2 oz
25 g	butter	1 oz
	salt and pepper	

Stud the onion with the cloves and place it in a bowl with the milk. Cover and cook on high for 5 [3½] minutes. Leave to stand for 15 minutes. Remove the onion and cloves, stir in the butter, breadcrumbs and season to taste. Reheat for 1-2 minutes if necessary. Serve with roast poultry.

Redcurrant Sauce

Cooking Time 7 [5] Minutes

Makes about 300 ml/½ pint

225 g	redcurrant jelly	8 oz
6 tbsp	dry cider	6 tbsp
3 tbsp	red wine vinegar	3 tbsp
2 tbsp	demerara sugar	2 tbsp
1 tsp	prepared mustard	1 tsp
40 g	raisins	1½ oz
	salt and pepper	

Combine the redcurrant jelly, cider, vinegar and sugar. Heat on high for 2 [1½] minutes to dissolve the jelly. Stir well, and cook on high for 5 [3½] minutes to reduce by a third. Stir in the remaining ingredients. Allow to cool and thicken. Serve with cold meat.

Easy

Chocolate Sauce

Cooking Time 2 [1½] Minutes

Makes 250 ml/8 fl oz

175 g	soft brown sugar	6 oz
50 g	butter	2 oz
1 tbsp	drinking chocolate	1 tbsp
2-3 tbsp	milk	2-3 tbsp

Combine all the ingredients. Cook on high for 2 [1½] minutes, stirring twice during cooking. Do not boil. Serve with ice cream or steamed pudding.

Easy

American Fudge Sauce

Cooking Time 3 [2½] Minutes

Makes about 250 ml/8 fl oz

5 tbsp	single cream	5 tbsp
25 g	cocoa	1 oz
100 g	caster sugar	4 oz
175 g	golden syrup	6 oz
25 g	butter	1 oz
½ tsp	vanilla essence	½ tsp

Combine all the ingredients except the vanilla. Cook on high for 3 [2½] minutes, stirring twice during the cooking. Add the vanilla essence. Cool a little before serving with ice cream or profiteroles.

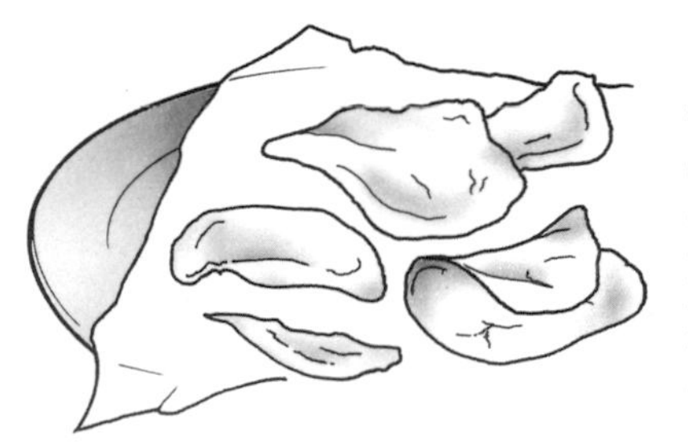

Microtip

To crisp up crackers or crisps which have softened, place them in a dish with absorbent kitchen paper and microwave on high for 30-60 [20-40] seconds.

PUDDINGS AND DESSERTS

Once you own a microwave oven there is no real excuse for cutting out the dessert course of a meal. Traditional puddings which are so time consuming to prepare conventionally can be cooked in only minutes in the microwave — steamed puddings, suet puddings, rice pudding and egg custard dishes are just a few examples.
Fresh fruit and frozen fruits can be cooked and like vegetables retain a good colour and superb flavour. Allow approximately 6 [4] minutes on high, per 450 g/1 lb of fresh fruit. Frozen fruits such as raspberries and strawberries can be defrosted to just the right amount of softness in a very few minutes. Dried fruits too can be cooked without soaking overnight. To stew dried apricots, peaches and pears use 225 g/8 oz fruit plus 600 ml/1 pint water, cook for 10 [7] minutes on high. Stand for 10 minutes. Prunes need 5 minutes longer for both cooking and standing times.
custards and making sponge bases for gateaux are just some of the ways in which your microwave will be more efficient than conventional cooking.
Fruit pies are best cooked conventionally, as the fillings cook quicker than the pastry and can ooze out, but they can be reheated very successfully or defrosted from the freezer.

Chocolate Sponge Pudding with Chocolate Sauce page 75
Mincemeat Pudding page 75
Lemon Syrup Pudding page 78

Easy

Rice Pudding

Cooking Time 27-28 [19] Minutes Serves 4

75 g	short grain rice	3 oz
600 ml	milk	1 pint
¼ tsp	salt	¼ tsp
40 g	sugar	1½ oz
40 g	butter	1½ oz
1 tbsp	brown sugar	1 tbsp
	pinch of nutmeg	

Into a buttered, deep pudding dish put the rice, milk, salt and sugar. Cook, uncovered on high for 7-8 [5] minutes, stir well and continue to cook, uncovered on medium for 20 [14] minutes. Leave to stand for 10 [7] minutes. To serve pour over melted butter 60 [40] seconds on high and sprinkle with the brown sugar and nutmeg.

Easy

Apple Crumble

Cooking Time 10 [7] Minutes Serves 4

675 g	cooking apples, peeled, cored and sliced	1½ lb
175 g	demerara sugar	6 oz
2 tsp	ground ginger	2 tsp
2 tbsp	orange juice	2 tbsp
175 g	plain flour	6 oz
75 g	butter or margarine	3 oz

Place the apple slices in a shallow buttered dish. Sprinkle them with half the sugar, half the ginger, and the orange juice. Rub flour and butter or margarine together until the mixture resembles breadcrumbs. Add the remaining sugar and ginger and press the mixture down firmly on the apple slices. Cook, uncovered on high for 10 [7]* minutes. Stand for 5 minutes.

* For 800 watt ovens cook for 6 minutes on high.

Apple Crunch

Cooking Time 9 [7] Minutes Serves 4

450 g	cooking apples peeled, cored and sliced	1 lb
25 g	sugar	1 oz
	pinch of cinnamon	
1	egg yolk	1
25 g	cornflour	1 oz
1 level tbsp	sugar	1 level tbsp
300 ml	milk	½ pint
40 g	butter	1½ oz
75 g	rolled oats	3 oz
40 g	brown sugar	1½ oz

Combine apples, sugar, cinnamon in a 600 ml/1 pint ovenproof dish. Cover and cook on high for 4 [3] minutes. Beat egg yolk and cornflour together and stir in sugar. Warm milk on high for 2 [1½] minutes and pour onto cornflour, stirring well. Cook uncovered on high for 2 [1½] minutes until thickened. Stir well. Remove cover from apples and pour over the custard.

In a separate bowl, melt the butter on high for 60 [40] seconds. Stir in the rolled oats and brown sugar and scatter over the custard. If desired this can be grilled for a few minutes for a crisp golden top. Serve hot or cold.

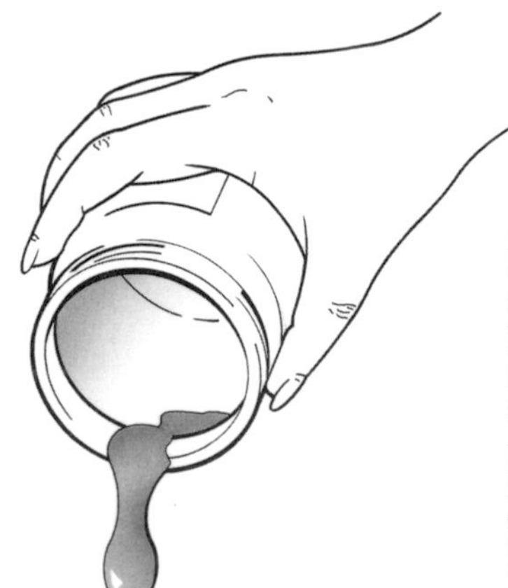

Microtip

Place almost empty jars of honey or syrup, with lids removed, in the microwave on high for 20-30 [15-25] seconds — you will be surprised at how much this will yield. Crystallised honey will also soften in the microwave on high for 60 [40] seconds.

Timings given are for 650 [750-800] watt ovens

Mincemeat Pudding

Cooking Time 4-5 [3] Minutes Serves 4

5 rounded tbsp	*mincemeat*	*5 rounded tbsp*
25 g	*glace cherries, chopped*	*1 oz*
100 g	*margarine*	*4 oz*
100 g	*caster sugar*	*4 oz*
2	*eggs*	*2*
175 g	*self raising flour*	*6 oz*
2 tbsp	*milk*	*2 tbsp*

Combine the chopped cherries and mincemeat and spoon into the base of a greased 1.15 litre/2 pint basin. Cream remaining ingredients together and turn into basin. Cook, uncovered, on high for 4-5 [3] minutes. Stand for 5 minutes before turning onto a plate. Serve with custard.

Sponge Pudding with Apricot Sauce

Cooking time 5 [3½] minutes Serves 4

3	*eggs, separated*	*3*
3 tbsp	*honey*	*3 tbsp*
	grated rind and juice of 1 orange	
50 g	*wholemeal flour*	*2 oz*
75 g	*currants*	*3 oz*
225 g can	*apricots*	*7½-8 oz can*

Whisk egg yolks, honey and orange rind until thick and creamy. Beat in orange juice and fold in the flour and currants.

Whisk egg whites until stiff and fold into mixture. Liquidise apricots and juice and spoon 4-5 tablespoons into a greased 1¼ litre (2 pint) basin, cover with the mixture and cook uncovered on high for 5 [3½]* minutes. Stand for 5 minutes before turning out. Heat remaining apricot puree for 2-3 [1½-2] minutes on high and serve with pudding.

* For 800 watt ovens cook for 3 minutes on high.

Easy

Chocolate Sponge Pudding with Chocolate Sauce

Cooking Time Pudding 4-5 [3] Minutes

Sauce 3 [2½] Minutes Serves 4

100 g	*margarine*	*4 oz*
100 g	*caster sugar*	*4 oz*
90 g	*self raising flour*	*3½ oz*
15 g	*cocoa*	*½ oz*
2	*eggs*	*2*
	Chocolate Sauce	
25 g	*butter*	*1 oz*
75 g	*soft brown sugar*	*3 oz*
2 tbsp	*cocoa*	*2 tbsp*
2 tbsp	*milk*	*2 tbsp*
1 tsp	*vanilla essence*	*1 tsp*

Grease a 1.15 litre/2 pint pudding basin. Cream together the margarine, sugar, flour, cocoa and eggs; add 1-2 tablespoons water to make a fairly liquid mixture. Turn into the basin and cook, uncovered on high for 4-5 [3] minutes. Stand for 5 minutes before turning out onto a serving dish.

To make the sauce, melt the butter on high for 60 [40] seconds. Stir in the remaining ingredients and cook uncovered on high for 2 [1½] minutes. Stir well and pour over pudding.

Timings given are for 650 [750-800] watt ovens

Chocolate Mandarin Cheesecake page 81
Black Cherry Flan page 82

Christmas Pudding page 83
Festive Mincemeat Flan page 83
Rich Fruit Cake page 88
Christmas Punch page 98

Easy

Jam Roly-Poly

Cooking Time 6 [4-4½] Minutes Serves 4

150 g	self-raising flour	6 oz
	pinch of salt	
75 g	suet	3 oz
6 tbsp	hot water	6 tbsp
6 tbsp	jam	6 tbsp
1 tbsp	lemon juice	1 tbsp

Combine the flour, salt and suet in a mixing bowl and bind together with the hot water. Knead lightly and roll out to an oblong approximately 36 cm x 18 cm/14" x 7". Spread half the jam to within ½" of edges and roll up lengthwise. Place on a plate and shape into a ring. Cover with a piece of greaseproof paper and cook on high for 5 [3-3½] minutes. Stand for 3-4 minutes before serving with jam sauce.

To make sauce, combine lemon juice with remaining jam and cook on high for 60 [40] seconds, stir and serve poured over roly-poly.

Easy

Baked Egg Custard

Cooking Time 14 [11½] Minutes Serves 4

300 ml	milk	½ pint
3	eggs	3
1	egg yolk	1
75 g	caster sugar	3 oz
½ tsp	vanilla essence	½ tsp
	pinch of nutmeg	

Warm the milk on high for 2 [1½] minutes in a 600 ml/1 pint straight sided dish. Beat together the eggs and egg yolk and strain into the milk. Stir in the sugar and vanilla and sprinkle with nutmeg. Cover and cook on medium setting for 12 [10] minutes or until the custard is set. Stand for 10 minutes before serving.

Easy

Lemon Syrup Pudding

Cooking Time 4-4½ [3] Minutes Serves 4

3 tbsp	golden syrup	3 tbsp
1	egg	1
6 tbsp	milk	6 tbsp
100 g	self raising flour	4 oz
50 g	caster sugar	2 oz
50 g	suet	2 oz
	grated rind of 1 lemon	

Grease a 1.15 litre/2 pint pudding basin. Spread the syrup in the bottom. Beat the egg and milk together. Combine the remaining ingredients; add the egg mixture and pour into the basin. Cover the basin with greaseproof paper and cook on high for 4 [2½] minutes. Stand for 5 minutes before turning out onto a serving dish.

Variation: Jam Sponge Pudding — replace syrup with 4 tablespoons raspberry jam and cook for 4½ [3] minutes.

Easy

Cider Baked Apples

Cooking Time 7-8 [5-6] Serves 4

4	medium cooking apples, cored but left whole	4
50 g	mixed dried fruit	2 oz
25 g	brown sugar	1 oz
50 g	butter	2 oz
150 ml	cider	¼ pint

Slit the skin around the middle of each apple and place in suitable serving dish. Combine the sugar and dried fruit and use it to stuff the cavity in the apples left by removing the core. Pour cider over apples and top each apple with a knob of butter. Cover and cook on high for 7-8 [5-6] minutes. Leave to stand for 5 minutes before serving. Serve with pouring cream.

Variation: Substitute dried fruit and sugar with "no cook" dried apricots chopped up and combined with a little honey.

Timings given are for 650 [750-800] watt ovens

Apricot Mousses

Cooking Time 2½-3½ [2] Minutes Serves 4-6

1 tbsp	custard powder	1 tbsp
2 level tbsp	sugar	2 level tbsp
150 ml	milk	¼ pint
2 tsp	gelatine	2 tsp
	grated rind and juice of 1 lemon	
425 g can	drained apricots — pureed	15 oz can
150 ml	double cream — whipped	¼ pint
6 tbsp	raspberry puree	6 tbsp

Blend custard powder and sugar with the milk in a jug and cook on high for 2-3 [1½-2] minutes stirring once during cooking and at the end. Sprinkle gelatine onto lemon juice to soften and dissolve on high for 30 [20] seconds. Stir the dissolved gelatine, lemon rind and apricot puree into the custard and leave to cool. Fold in the whipped cream and spoon half the mixture into the bottom of wine glasses and chill in the refrigerator to set. Spoon on half of the raspberry puree and cover with the remaining apricot custard. Swirl over the surface the remaining raspberry puree and chill to serve.

Easy

Gingernut Creams

Cooking Time 5 [4] Minutes Serves 4-6

2 level tbsp	sugar	2 level tbsp
3 level tbsp	cornflour	3 level tbsp
450 ml	milk	¾pint
	grated rind of 1 lemon	
2	eggs, separated	2
100 g	crushed ginger biscuits	4 oz
	a little ground cinnamon	

Combine sugar and cornflour in a jug and blend with a little of the milk. Stir in the rest of the milk. Cook on high for 5 [4] minutes stirring twice, until thickened. Beat in egg yolks and rind. Cover with cooking film to prevent skin forming and leave to cool. Whisk egg whites to soft peaks and fold into mixture. Scatter ginger biscuit crumbs in the base of wine glasses and pour over the mixture. Chill to set. Serve with a light dusting of ground cinnamon.

Orange Charlotte

Cooking Time 6 [4-4½] Minutes Serves 4-6

15 g	gelatine	½ oz
	grated rind and juice of 1 orange	
300 ml	milk	½ pint
2	eggs — separated	2
50 g	caster sugar	2 oz
150 ml	orange yogurt	5 fl oz
15	sponge fingers	15
	a little extra milk	
150 ml	double cream, whipped	¼ pint
	orange slices for decoration	

Sprinkle gelatine over orange juice and dissolve on high for 40 [30] seconds, stir to dissolve. Heat milk and orange rind on high for 3 [2] minutes. Beat egg yolks and sugar together until creamy. Pour the hot milk on to the eggs stirring well. Cook uncovered on high for 2 [1½] minutes, stir well.

Stir gelatine into custard, cover with film and leave to cool. Line the sides and base of a 15 cm/6" loose bottom tin with greaseproof paper. Dip sides of sponge fingers into extra milk and stand side by side around edge of tin, sugar side out. When custard is on the point of set, stir in the yogurt. Whisk egg whites until stiff and fold into the mixture. Pour into tin and leave to set. Trim biscuits level with set mixture if necessary and turn out on to a serving plate. Decorate with whirls of fresh cream and orange slices.

Timings given are for 650 [750-800] watt ovens

Apricot Mousses page 79
Orange Charlotte page 79

Chocolate Mandarin Cheesecake

Cooking Time 2½ [1½] Minutes Serves 4-6

	Base	
175 g	*crushed digestive biscuits*	*6 oz*
50 g	*plain chocolate*	*2 oz*
50 g	*butter*	*2 oz*
	Filling	
15 g	*gelatine*	*½ oz*
	grated rind and juice of 1 lemon	
	grated rind and juice of 1 orange	
50 g	*dried milk powder*	*2 oz*
175 g	*caster sugar*	*6 oz*
225 g	*full cream cheese*	*8 oz*
275 g	*can mandarin oranges*	*10 oz*
	decoration	
150 ml	*whipping cream*	*5 fl oz*
	a little melted chocolate	

To make the base, combine the chocolate and butter and melt uncovered, on high for 1½ [1] minutes. Stir to dissolve then fold in biscuit crumbs, press into the base of an 8" loose-bottom cake tin and chill to set.

For the filling, sprinkle the gelatine on to the lemon juice to soften and dissolve on high for 40 [30] seconds, stir well and leave to cool. Add the juice from the mandarin oranges to the orange juice and make up to 300 ml/½ pint with water. In a food processor or blender, combine the orange and lemon rind, milk powder, caster sugar and cream cheese, add the water and orange juice gradually until well blended. Add the dissolved gelatine and pour on to the biscuit base and chill, to set.

While the cheesecake is setting, dip the mandarin segments halfway into the melted chocolate to coat and leave to set on greaseproof paper. To decorate the cheesecake, whip the cream and pipe around the edge. Decorate with the half-dipped chocolate oranges.

Blackberry and Apple Flan

Cooking Time 8 [5½] Minutes Serves 4-6

	Biscuit Base	
175 g	*digestive biscuits, crushed*	*6 oz*
1 tbsp	*syrup*	*1 tbsp*
50 g	*margarine*	*2 oz*
	Filling	
1	*large cooking apple, peeled, cored and sliced*	*1*
225 g	*blackberries*	*8 oz*
50 g	*sugar*	*2 oz*
	Topping	
150 ml	*plain yogurt*	*5 fl oz*
100 g	*cream cheese*	*4 oz*
1 level tbsp	*gelatine*	*1 level tbsp*
3 tbsp	*water*	*3 tbsp*
	grated rind and juice of 1 lemon	

For the base, combine syrup and butter or margarine and melt on high for 50 [40] seconds, stir in biscuit crumbs and press into a flan case.

For the filling combine the fruit and sugar, reserve some berries for decoration, cover and cook on high for 6 [4] minutes . Allow to cool then transfer fruit with a draining spoon to flan case and chill.

For the topping, sprinkle gelatine onto water and dissolve on high for 40 [30] seconds. Blend cream cheese and yogurt together, stir in lemon rind, juice and dissolved gelatine, pour over the fruit and chill to set. Decorate with reserved berries to serve.

NB The filling can be substituted with a can of pie filling.

Timings given are for 650 [750-800] watt ovens

Black Cherry Flan

Cooking Time 6½-7½ [5-5½] Minutes Serves 4-6

	Flan Base	
2	eggs	2
50 g	caster sugar	2 oz
40 g	self-raising flour	1½ oz
1½ level tbsp	cocoa	1½ level tbsp
	Filling	
1x450 ml can	black cherries	1x15 oz can
3 level tsp	arrowroot	3 level tsp
150 ml	double cream — whipped	5 fl oz

Warm sugar in a bowl for 2 [1½] minutes on high. Break in the eggs and whisk until thickened. Sieve flour and cocoa and fold into whisked eggs with a metal spoon until evenly blended. Pour into a greased flan dish for microwave use and cook on high for 2½-3 [2] minutes. Stand for 5 minutes before turning out onto plain kitchen paper on a wire rack to cool.

Drain the juice from the cherries and reserve. Blend a little juice into arrowroot until smooth, stir in remainder and cook on high for 2-3 [1½-2] minutes, stirring halfway through cooking. When thickened, stir in drained cherries, leave to cool. Spoon cherry mixture into flan case, and pipe whipped cream around edge to serve.

Old English Trifle

Cooking Time 11 [8½] Minutes Serves 8

600 ml	milk, warmed	1 pint
2-3 drops	vanilla essence	2-3 drops
2	eggs	2
2	egg yolks	2
2 tbsp	caster sugar	2 tbsp
25 g	cornflour	1 oz
8	trifle sponges	8
1 (225 g)	can apricots, drained and pureed	1 (8 oz)
100 g	macaroons, lightly crushed	4 oz
6 tbsp	medium sherry	6 tbsp
300 ml	whipping cream	½ pint
50 g	flaked almonds	2 oz

Blend the eggs, egg yolks and sugar into the cornflour. Warm the milk on high for 3 [2] minutes then stir into the egg mixture. Heat on high for 2½ [2] minutes stirring twice. Spread trifle sponges with the apricot puree. Cover the sponges with the crushed macaroons and then pour the sherry over them. Add custard and spread evenly. Leave to cool and set. Whip the cream and spread it over the custard. Place the flaked almonds on a plate and toast on high for 6 [4] minutes until golden brown. Allow to cool then sprinkle them over the cream.

NB: If you like, use extra whipped cream to pipe cream whirls. This trifle is greatly improved if allowed to chill in a refrigerator for at least 4 hours or overnight.

Microtip

Dissolve a jelly tablet by placing the whole piece in a measuring jug. Microwave on high for 60 [40] seconds, stir well until dissolved then add the required amount of cold water (or ice cubes and water) and stir. Chill to set.

Timings given are for 650 [750-800] watt ovens

Christmas Pudding

Cooking Time Small x 2 60-65 [40-45] Minutes
Large x 1 65-70 [45-50] Minutes Serves 8-10

50 g	self-raising flour	2 oz
100 g	white breadcrumbs	4 oz
½ tsp	mixed spice	½ tsp
½ tsp	cinnamon	½ tsp
½ tsp	nutmeg	½ tsp
1	grated carrot	1
1	grated apple	1
	grated rind and juice of 1 lemon	
675 g	mixed dried fruit	1½ lb
75 g	dark brown sugar	3 oz
	grated rind of 1 orange	
75 g	melted butter	3 oz
1 tbsp	black treacle	1 tbsp
2	eggs	2
150 ml	stout	¼ pint

Combine all the ingredients well together and turn into a greased 1.15 ml/2 pint basin or divide between two greased 600 ml/1 pint basins. Cover and cook the small puddings together on medium low for 60-65 [40-45]* minutes or cook the large pudding on medium low for 65-70 [45-50]* minutes. Leave both sizes to stand for 5-20 minutes before turning them out, if using straight away.

If using plastic pudding basins check they will withstand a high heat as the mixture is high in sugar and fat and becomes very hot. This can cause some plastics to buckle during cooking.

To store the puddings, cool and wrap well in foil. To serve, remove the foil and reheat on medium high setting for 3-4 [2-3] minutes for a small one and 4-5 [3] minutes for the large pudding.

* For 800 watt ovens cook small puddings for 34-36 minutes and large pudding for 30-34 minutes, on medium low.

Easy

Festive Mincemeat Flan

Cooking Time 3-5 [2½-3½] Minutes Serves 8

225g	digestive biscuits, crushed	8 oz
50 g	margarine	2 oz
2 tbsp	golden syrup	2 tbsp
1 (440 g)	can pear halves	1 (15½ oz)
2 level tbsp	custard powder	2 level tbsp
2 tbsp	mincemeat	2 tbsp
1 tsp	lemon juice	1 tsp
	glace cherries	

Melt the margarine with the golden syrup on high for 1-2 [¾-1½] minutes and combine with biscuit crumbs. Press into the bottom and sides of a flan ring or dish. Chill to set.

Drain the pears and make liquid up to 150 ml/¼ pint with water if necessary. Blend the liquid into the custard powder and cook on high for 2-3 [1½-2] minutes, stirring twice during cooking. Add the mincemeat and lemon juice and spoon into the flan case. Smooth the surface and arrange the pear halves — cut side down with narrow end towards the centre, and decorate with glace cherries. Serve hot or cold.

Baked Bananas *Easy*

Cooking Time 3½-4½ [3] Minutes Serves 2

25 g	butter	1 oz
1 tbsp	soft brown sugar	1 tbsp
2	bananas, peeled	2
1 tbsp	rum or brandy (optional)	1 tbsp

Combine the butter and sugar and cook on high for 1-2 [¾-1½] minutes, to melt butter. Stir in the rum or brandy, if using. Add bananas, whole, to the sauce and baste well. Cover and cook on high for 2½ [1½-2] minutes. Serve with ice cream or fresh cream.

Timings given are for 650 [750-800] watt ovens

Oranges in Caramel

Cooking Time 14-17 [12½-14] Minutes Serves 4-6

8	oranges	8
225 g	granulated sugar	8 oz
150 ml	water	¼ pint
1 tbsp	liqueur or brandy	1 tbsp
150 ml	hot water	¼ pint

Grate the rind of 3 of the oranges and reserve it. Remove the skin and pith from all the oranges and slice thinly, putting each one back together and securing with a cocktail stick.

Stir the sugar into the cold water and any surplus orange juice, cook on high for 2-3 [1½-2] minutes and stir to completely dissolve the sugar. Boil in the microwave oven on high for 12-14 [11-12] minutes without stirring until it turns golden brown. Quickly stir in hot water and liqueur, or brandy. Leave to cool. Pour the liquid over the oranges and chill. Serve sprinkled with grated rind.

Creme Caramel

Cooking Time 14 [9½-10½] Minutes Serves 4-6

1	quantity egg custard (page 78)	1
6 tbsp	water	6 tbsp
100 g	granulated sugar	4 oz

Combine the water and sugar in a 600 ml/1 pint ovenproof souffle dish. Cook on high for 2 [1½] minutes and stir until the sugar has dissolved. Cook, uncovered on high for 12 [8-9] minutes until the syrup has turned golden brown. Allow to cool, then pour the egg custard over the caramel. Cook as for baked egg custard. Leave to cool, then chill well. To serve, invert on a serving dish.

Apricot Snow

Cooking Time 6 [4] minutes Serves 4-6

350 g	cooking apples, peeled, cored and sliced	12 oz
	grated rind and juice of 1 lemon	
75 g	sugar	3 oz
400 g	can of apricots	14 oz
2 tbsp	apricot brandy or Grand Marnier	2 tbsp
2	egg whites	2
2 tsp	caster sugar	2 tsp

Combine apple slices, lemon juice and two tablespoons of the apricot jam in a covered dish. Cook on high for 6 [4] minutes until very soft. Turn into a blender or food processor with sugar and drained apricots. Process to a pulp then add liquer. Whisk egg whites until firm, whisk in two teaspoons of caster sugar and fold into the apricot mixture. Pour into individual glass dishes and chill to set. Serve decorated with chopped nuts.

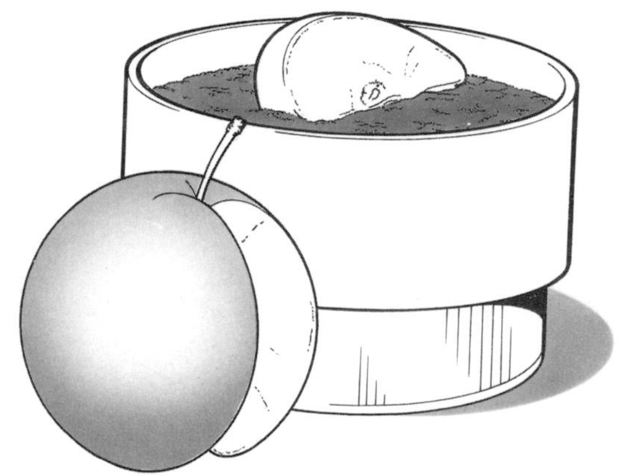

Microtip

To soften brown sugar when it has become hard, add an apple wedge to the sugar and microwave on high for 30-40 [20-30] seconds. Leave it stand for a few minutes before removing the apple.

Blackcurrant Delight

Cooking Time 1½ [1] Minutes Serves 4-6

	biscuit base	
175 g	crushed digestive biscuits	6 oz
1 tbsp	syrup	1 tbsp
50 g	margarine or butter	2 oz
	filling	
300 g can	blackcurrants	10½ oz can
½	blackcurrant jelly	½
150 ml	plain yogurt	5 fl oz
100 g	low fat cream cheese	4 oz

For the biscuit base, melt margarine or butter and syrup on high for 50 [40] seconds, stir in the biscuit crumbs. Turn into a flan dish and press into base, chill to firm.

For the filling dissolve the jelly in a measuring jug, on high for 30 [20] seconds, stir well. Drain the juice from the blackcurrants into the jelly and make up to 300 ml/½ pint with water if necessary. Leave until point of setting.

Meanwhile blend the cream cheese and yogurt together until smooth, fold in the drained blackcurrants reserving some for decoration. Stir in the jelly when just about to set and turn into flan case. Chill to set and serve decorated with reserved berries.

Easy

Golden Fruit Pudding

Cooking Time 5-6 [4] Minutes Serves 4

1	large cooking apple, peeled, cored and diced	1
75 g	mixed dried fruit	3 oz
4	glace cherries, chopped	4
1 tbsp	chopped dates	1 tbsp
1 tbsp	demerara sugar	1 tbsp
½ tsp	ground cinnamon	½ tsp
50 g	soft margarine	2 oz
50 g	sugar	2 oz
75 g	self raising flour	3 oz
½ tsp	baking powder	½ tsp
1	egg	1
1 tbsp	milk	1 tbsp

Grease a 1.15 litre/2 pint pudding basin. Combine the fruit, demerara sugar and cinnamon and reserve. Mix together the margarine, sugar, flour, baking powder, egg and milk. Put half the fruit mixture in the bottom of the basin. Cover with half the sponge mixture; repeat the layers. Cook on high for 5-6 [4] minutes, uncovered. Stand for 5 minutes before turning out. Serve warm with custard.

Pineapple Creams

Cooking Time 6-7 [4-5] Minutes Serves 4-6

425 g can	pineapple pieces	15 oz can
50 g	cornflour	2 oz
100 g	sugar	4 oz
2 tbsp	lemon juice	2 tbsp
300 ml	double cream	½ pint

Drain pineapples and make up to 600 ml/1 pint with water. blend a little of the liquid with the cornflour and sugar then add the rest of the liquid. Cook, uncovered, on high for 6-7 [4-5] minutes, stirring twice during cooking, until thickened. Stir in lemon juice and cover with cooking film to prevent skin forming. Leave to cool. Whip cream until thick and fold into the cooled sauce. Stir in pineapple pieces and turn into individual dishes. Chill to serve.

Timings given are for 650 [750-800] watt ovens

BAKING

Cakes will not brown in a microwave oven, though this is an advantage with certain kinds of cake, such as angel cake and cheesecake. However, cakes must be removed from the oven while the top is still moist, as cooking will continue during standing time. If left in the oven until the top is dry, when cooled the cake will be too dry. Most cake mixtures need to be rather softer than usual so add a little water to your favourite recipe.

Metal cake containers cannot be used but you can create unusual shaped baking dishes by lining suitable kitchen containers or cardboard boxes with greaseproof paper or plain kitchen roll. Cake cases are useful for individual cakes or for a conventional round cake shape a large souffle dish is suitable. Jelly moulds or plastic moulds also produce attractive cakes.

Using brown sugar and flours and treacle where appropriate helps to give colour to cakes. Plain cakes can be sprinkled with sifted sugar or covered with glace icing. Rich fruit cakes need to be cooked on medium low setting. This allows the flavours to develop and the colour to deepen, giving you a moist, evenly coloured cake.

Bread making can be speeded up by letting the dough rise in the microwave oven. Cover and give short blasts of 10-15 seconds on high, resting for 15 minutes and repeating until the dough has doubled in bulk.

Bread can also be baked in the microwave oven though this will give a soft bread. For a crusty brown top, finish under a moderate grill for 2-3 minutes.

Gingerbread

Cooking Time 4½-5 [3½] Minutes Serves 6

50 g	butter	2 oz
25 g	brown sugar	1 oz
2 tbsp	treacle	2 tbsp
100 g	plain flour	4 oz
½ tsp	bicarbonate of soda	½ tsp
1 tsp	ground ginger	1 tsp
1	egg	1

Combine the butter, sugar and treacle in a mixing bowl and cook on high for 90 [60] seconds. Stir well to melt the butter. Leave the mixture to cool slightly. Stir in the dry ingredients then beat in the egg. Pour into a greased 1.4 litre/2½ pint loaf dish. Shield across both ends of the dish with a strip of foil and cook, uncovered, on high for 3-3½ [2½] minutes. Leave to stand for 5 minutes; turn out to cool. Serve sliced and buttered.

Easy

Lemon Sponge

Cooking Time 5-6 [4-5] Minutes Serves 8-10

175 g	soft margarine	6 oz
175 g	caster sugar	6 oz
3	eggs	3
175 g	self raising flour	6 oz
	grated rind of 1 lemon	
2 tbsp	water	2 tbsp
4 tbsp	lemon curd	4 tbsp
2 tbsp	icing sugar, sifted	2 tbsp

Cream the margarine and sugar until light and fluffy. Beat in the eggs, fold in the flour and lemon rind. Add enough water to make a soft mixture. Divide mixture between two cake dishes suitable for the microwave oven. Cook each separately on high for 2½-3 [2-2½] minutes; the top of the sponge should still be moist. Leave to stand for 5 minutes before turning out onto kitchen paper on a wire rack. When cool, sandwich the cakes together with the lemon curd and dredge the top with icing sugar

Easy

Easy Make Chocolate Sponge

Cooking Time 5 [4] Minutes Serves 8-10

175 g	soft margarine	6 oz
175 g	caster sugar	6 oz
150 g	self raising flour	5 oz
25 g	cocoa powder	1 oz
1 tsp	baking powder	1 tsp
3	eggs	3
2-3 tbsp	water	2-3 tbsp
4 tbsp	chocolate butter cream	4 tbsp
2 tbsp	icing sugar, sifted	2 tbsp

Combine the margarine, sugar, flour, cocoa, baking powder and eggs with 2 tablespoons of water in a large mixing bowl. Mix well, but do not overbeat. You need a rather more liquid mixture than for conventional sponges, so add the remaining water if necessary. Divide the mixture between two greased 17.5 ml/7" cake containers and cook each separately for 2½ [2] minutes on high. Leave each one to stand for 5 minutes, then turn out onto absorbent kitchen paper covering a wire rack, and leave to cool. Sandwich together with the butter cream and sprinkle the top with the icing sugar.

Timings given are for 650 [750-800] watt ovens

Easy

Small Sponge Cakes

Cooking Time 3-4 [2-3] minutes Makes 12

50 g	*soft margarine*	*2 oz*
50 g	*caster sugar*	*2 oz*
1	*size 3 egg*	*1*
100 g	*self raising flour*	*4 oz*
2-4 tbsp	*milk*	*2-4 tbsp*

Cream the margarine and sugar together until light and fluffy. Beat in the egg and then fold in the flour with the milk to form a soft dropping consistency. Alternatively put all ingredients into a food processor and mix until smooth.

Place double paper cases into a 6 hole bun tray or teacups or ramekin dishes. Half fill the cases with the mixture and cook 6 at a time arranged in a ring, on high for 1½-2 [1-1½] minutes until the surfaces are only just dry. Leave to cool while cooking remaining cakes.

These cakes can be decorated with chocolate drops by arranging on surface of cakes immediately they are cooked. As the chocolate drops soften they will stick to the cakes when cooled.

Variations: *Lemon or orange cakes*: add the grated rind of 1 lemon or orange to mixture.
Coffee: 2 teaspoons instant coffee dissolved in 1 tablespoon hot water, in place of 1 tablespoon milk.
Chocolate: 1 tablespoon sifted into flour.

Microtip

If you do not have a ring mould place a glass or jar in the centre of a large souffle dish or round cake dish.

Rich Fruit Cake

Cooking Time 50 [35] Minutes
Makes 1 (20cm/8") cake

175 g	*butter*	*6 oz*
175 g	*soft brown sugar*	*6 oz*
3	*eggs*	*3*
1 tbsp	*treacle*	*1 tbsp*
175 g	*plain flour*	*6 oz*
225 g	*seedless raisins*	*8 oz*
225 g	*sultanas*	*8 oz*
225 g	*currants*	*8 oz*
25 g	*mixed peel*	*1 oz*
75 g	*glace cherries*	*3 oz*
1-2 tbsp	*brandy*	*1-2 tbsp*
	grated rind and juice of 1 lemon	
¼ tsp	*salt*	*¼ tsp*
¾ tsp	*ground mixed spice*	*¾ tsp*

Cream the butter and sugar together until pale and soft. Beat in the eggs one at a time adding the treacle and a tablespoon of flour. Mix together the fruit, with a tablespoon of flour. Fold the remaining flour into the mixture then add the fruit and all remaining ingredients. Line the base of a 20 cm/8" souffle dish with a circle of greaseproof paper then grease well. Turn the cake mixture into the dish. Smooth surface until flat. Cook uncovered on medium low for 50 [35]* minutes. Leave to stand for 30 minutes before turning out of dish.

This cake is better wrapped in foil and stored a few days before using. It will keep for several weeks and is ideal for Christmas.

* For 800 watt ovens cook for 30 minutes on medium low.

Easy

Apricot Fruit Loaf

Cooking Time 15-16 [10½-11½] Minutes

65 g	margarine	2½ oz
65 g	dark brown sugar	2½ oz
100 g	self raising flour	4 oz
¼ level tsp	mixed spice	¼ level tsp
¼ level tsp	cinnamon	¼ level tsp
1	egg	1
1 dsrt spoon	black treacle	1 dsrt spoon
50 g	dried apricots	2 oz
150 ml	water	¼ pint
100 g	mixed dried fruit	4 oz
3 tbsp	milk	3 tbsp

Put apricots and water in a bowl and microwave on high for 2 [1½] minutes and leave to stand for 20-30 minutes. Strain and reserve juice. Chop apricots.

Mix all remaining ingredients well together and stir in apricots and enough reserved juice to make a soft mixture. Turn into a greased 1 lb loaf shape container suitable for microwave. Cook on medium power for 13-14 [9-10]* minutes. Leave to stand for 5-10 minutes before turning out. Mix a little glace icing and drizzle across the top of the cake and decorate with slivers of apricot.

* For 800 watt ovens cook for 8 minutes on medium power.

Easy

Wholemeal Chocolate Cake

Cooking Time 6½ [4½] Minutes

	Cake	
100 g	margarine	4 oz
100 g	soft dark brown sugar	4 oz
2	eggs, beaten	2
100 g	wholemeal flour	4 oz
2 tbsp	carob powder	2 tbsp
2 tsp	baking powder	2 tsp
	pinch of salt	
2 tbsp	milk	2 tbsp
	Topping	
100 g	margarine	4 oz
2 tbsp	carob powder	2 tbsp
175 g	icing sugar	6 oz
4 tbsp	milk	4 tbsp

Cream margarine and sugar together, add beaten eggs. Fold in flour, carob powder, baking powder and salt. Add milk and turn into a 20 cm/8" round container. Cook on high for 4½ [3] minutes, stand for 5 minutes before turning out to cool. For topping, combine all ingredients in a bowl and cook on high for 2 [1½] minutes. Beat until smooth and leave to cool for 5 minutes. When cool, pour topping over the cake and smooth over top and sides evenly. Decorate with a little grated chocolate.

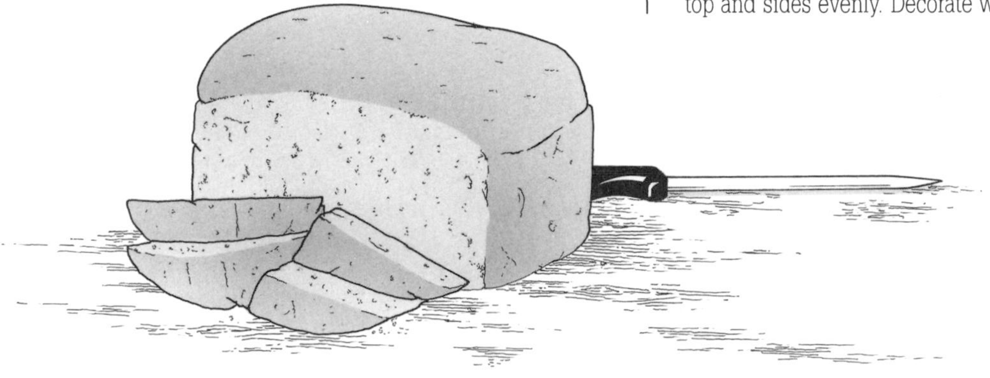

Timings given are for 650 [750-800] watt ovens

Easy Make Chocolate Sponge page 87

Apricot Fruit Loaf page 89
Flapjacks page 92

Flapjacks

Cooking Time 7½ [5¼] Minutes Makes 8

100 g	butter	4 oz
75 g	soft brown sugar	3 oz
3 tbsp	golden syrup	3 tbsp
	pinch of salt	
1 tsp	baking powder	1 tsp
225 g	rolled oats	8 oz

Place the butter and sugar in a bowl and heat on high for 1½ [1¼] minutes until the butter has melted. Stir in the syrup, salt and baking powder then add the rolled oats and mix well. Press the mixture into a greased 20 cm/8" shallow dish. Cook on high for 6 [4] minutes. Leave to stand for 15 minutes then cut into pieces.

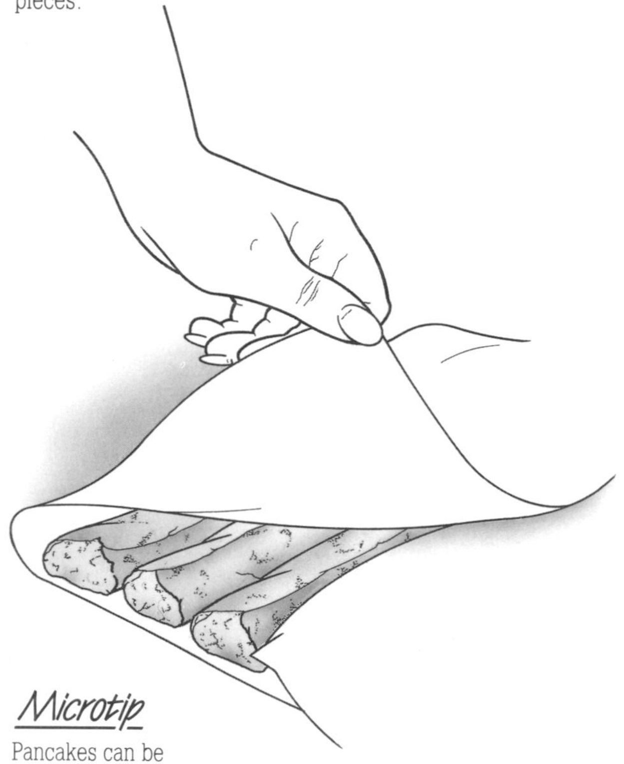

Microtip

Pancakes can be reheated by wrapping in a clean tea towel and microwaving on high. Eight will take about 2 [1½] minutes.

Easy

Bacon and Onion Scones

Cooking Time 4½ [3½] Minutes Makes 5

1	rasher rindless streaky bacon	1
25 g	margarine	1 oz
100 g	plain flour	4 oz
	pinch of salt	
	pinch of cayenne pepper	
½	onion grated or finely chopped	½
4 tbsp	milk	4 tbsp

Cook the bacon on high for 2 [1½] minutes until crisp, then crumble it. Rub the margarine into the flour until the mixture has the texture of breadcrumbs. Add salt, pepper and onion and bind with the milk. Shape into five rounds or squares. Place them in a ring on the turntable and cook on high for 2½ [2] minutes. Serve warm with butter.

Praline Topping

Cooking Time 5-8 [4-5½] Minutes Makes 175 g/6 oz.

50 g	whole almonds, unblanched	2 oz
100 g	granulated sugar	4 oz

Mix the almonds and sugar together on a sheet of non-stick baking paper or greaseproof paper. Cook on high for 5-8 [4-5½] minutes, stirring frequently until all the sugar has melted and caramelised. Leave until completely cooled. Put the praline in a liquidiser or food processor and grind to the required texture. Store in an air tight container. Use the topping for cakes or desserts or to sprinkle over ice cream.

PRESERVES AND DRINKS

Most of us appreciate homemade preserves and pickles but do not have the time to cope with the large amounts associated with conventional preserving methods. You will find your microwave oven quicker and cleaner and will be rewarded with a fresher taste and a better colour too as there is no risk of scorching.

As with conventional jam making it is beneficial to warm the sugar before using. This can be done by putting the sugar in a bag or a bowl and microwaving for 3-4 [2-3] minutes on high. It is important to make sure the sugar has dissolved with the fruit before letting it boil.

Jars can be sterilised in the microwave oven by filling them one-quarter to one-half full of water and bringing to the boil without lids (they may not necessarily all boil at the same time). Boil on high for 2-3 [1½-2] minutes. Under no circumstances must the jars be sealed as this could cause an explosion. Drain them and stand them upside down on kitchen paper. When the jars are filled with hot preserves cover the tops with cooking film and return them to the oven. Microwave on high for 1 minute, just until the film balloons up. Remove them from the oven and leave them to cool. The film will then shrink back forming a vacuum for storage.

PRESERVES AND DRINKS

Beverages can be made or reheated in the microwave. For milky drinks you can heat the drinks in their mugs. Allow room for expansion, avoid mugs or cups with glued on handles as some glues melt in the microwave. With autosensor ovens, you need only use the lowest setting as in most cases you do not require the beverages to boil. For a quick cup of tea, place the water in the cup or mug, bring to the boil on high then carefully add the tea or tea bag and stand for the desired time.

Lemon Curd

Cooking Time 450 g/1 lb 6-8 [4½-6] Minutes
900 g/2 lbs 10-11 [7-8] Minutes

	For 450 g/1 lb	
75 g	*butter*	*3 oz*
2	*eggs*	*2*
1	*egg yolk*	*1*
150 g	*caster sugar*	*5 oz*
	grated rind and juice of 2 lemons	
	For 900 g/2 lb	
175 g	*butter*	*6 oz*
4	*eggs*	*4*
2	*egg yolks*	*2*
275 g	*caster sugar*	*10 oz*
	grated rind and juice of 4 lemons	

Melt the butter on high for 2-3 [1½-2] minutes for 450 g/1 lb or 4 [3] minutes for 900 g/2 lb. Beat the eggs and yolks together and strain them on to the sugar, lemon juice and rind. Stir this into the hot butter. Cook on high for 4-5 [3-4] minutes for 450 g/1 lb or 6-7 [4-5] for 900 g/2 lb, stirring every minute until the mixture begins to thicken. Pour into sterilised jars and seal. Keep refrigerated.

NB: For lemon and lime curd replace half amount of lemons with limes. This curd is so quick and easy to make compared with conventional recipes and the flavour is superb.

Blackberry and Apple Curd

Cooking Time 14 [9½] Minutes

Makes 700-900 g/1½-2 lb

100 g	*cooking apple, sliced*	*4 oz*
225 g	*blackberries*	*8 oz*
40 g	*butter*	*1½ oz*
225 g	*caster sugar*	*8 oz*
	rind and juice of ½ lemon	
2	*eggs, beaten*	*2*

Cook apple and blackberries together in a covered container on high for 8 [5½] minutes until soft. Puree, then sieve the mixture to remove pips. Stir the butter, sugar, lemon rind and juice into the mixture until the butter melts. Strain the beaten eggs into the mixture, stir well then cook on high uncovered for 6 [4] minutes, stirring every minute, until it thickens. Pour into clean pots and seal.

Use as a preserve, filling for sponges or in desserts.

Lemon Curd page 94
Mixed Fruit Marmalade page 96
Strawberry Jam page 96

Mixed Fruit Marmalade

Cooking Time 20 [14] Minutes

Makes approximately 1.5 kg/3 lb

1	*grapefruit*	*1*
1	*orange*	*1*
1	*lemon*	*1*
450 ml	*boiling water*	*¾ pint*
900 g	*granulated sugar*	*2 lb*
25 g	*butter*	*1 oz*

Thinly pare the citrus fruit peel and reserve. Chop the flesh, including the pith, and put it into a large dish with the boiling water. Cook on high for 10 [7] minutes uncovered. Thinly slice the peel. Press the cooked pulp through a sieve. Discard what remains in the sieve. Stir the peel and sugar into the juice and cook on high for 10 [7] minutes, stir in the butter. Test a spoonful on a plate; if it does not wrinkle as it cools cook for another 2 minutes. Pour the jam into sterilised jars and seal.

Corn Pepper Relish

Cooking Time 6-7 [4½-5] Minutes

1	*green pepper, diced*	*1*
1	*red pepper, diced*	*1*
1	*small onion, chopped*	*1*
50 g	*frozen sweetcorn, thawed*	*2 oz*
2 tbsp	*demerara sugar*	*2 tbsp*
2 tbsp	*sherry*	*2 tbsp*
2 tbsp	*cider vinegar*	*2 tbsp*
	salt and pepper	

Combine the red and green peppers with the onion, cover and cook on high for 4 [3] minutes. Add remaining ingredients and cook on high for 2-3 [1½-2] minutes. Stand for 5 minutes, adjust seasoning to taste and serve hot or cold.

Strawberry Jam

Cooking Time 33 [25] minutes

Makes approximately 1.25 kg/2½ lb

1 kg	*strawberries*	*2 lb*
675 g	*sugar*	*1½ lb*
	juice of 1 lemon	

Combine the strawberries and lemon juice in a large oven proof bowl. Cover and cook on high for 8 [6] minutes stirring halfway. Stir in the sugar and cook, uncovered for 25 [19] minutes, until setting point is reached. Stir occasionally during the cooking. Leave the jam to cool a while before pouring into clean jars. Seal and label.

Tomato Chutney

Cooking Time 32-35 [23-27] Minutes

Makes 1.5 kg/3 lb

350 g	*tomatoes, skinned and chopped*	*12 oz*
350 g	*cooking apples, peeled, cored and chopped*	*12 oz*
1	*medium onion, chopped*	*1*
225 g	*raisins*	*8 oz*
2 tsp	*salt*	*2 tsp*
1 tsp	*ground ginger*	*1 tsp*
1 tsp	*dry mustard*	*1 tsp*
1	*clove garlic, crushed*	*1*
225 g	*brown sugar*	*8 oz*
450 ml	*malt vinegar*	*¾ pint*

Combine the tomatoes, apples and onions in a large bowl. Cover and cook on high for 10 [7] minutes, stirring halfway through the cooking. Add the remaining ingredients and mix well. Cook, uncovered, for 22-25 [16-20] minutes on high, depending on the ripeness of tomatoes, stirring several times during cooking. Cool slightly before pouring into warm sterilised jars. Seal and label.

Timings given are for 650 [750-800] watt ovens

Piccalilli

Cooking Time 14-16 [10-11½] Minutes

Makes about 1.2 kg/2¾ lbs

	Brine	
600 ml	cold water	1 pint
25 g	salt	1 oz
	Sauce	
600 ml	white wine vinegar	1 pint
3 tbsp	mustard powder	3 tbsp
2 tsp	ground ginger	2 tsp
1 tsp	turmeric	1 tsp
2 level tbsp	cornflour	2 level tbsp
	salt and pepper	
100 g	sugar	4 oz

Prepare approximately 900 g/2 lb fresh vegetables — such as cauliflower, courgettes, baby onions, mushrooms, green beans, cucumber, peppers, etc. and cut to a suitable size.

Dissolve the salt in water in a large bowl. Add the vegetables, cover and leave for 8 hours or overnight. Drain and dry vegetables on absorbent paper or a clean tea towel. Combine vegetables and 450 ml /¾ pint vinegar in a large bowl. Cover and cook on high for 10-12 [7-8½] minutes until vegetables are just cooked. Stir once during cooking.

Combine spices, cornflour, seasoning and blend in the remaining vinegar. Add to the vegetables with the sugar and stir well. Cook on high for 4 [3] minutes or until thickened, stir during cooking. Pour into clean jars and cover. Store in refrigerator for up to 4 weeks but leave for 10 days to mature before using.

Easy

Mincemeat

Cooking Time 6 [4] Minutes

Makes about 1.25 kg/2½ lbs

450 g	cooking apples, peeled, quartered and cored	1 lb
350 g	raisins	12 oz
175 g	currants	6 oz
175 g	sultanas	6 oz
25 g	mixed peel	1 oz
175 g	suet	6 oz
200 g	brown sugar	7 oz
	grated rind and juice of 1 lemon	
¼-½ tsp	mixed spice	¼-½ tsp
3 tbsp	brandy	3 tbsp

Place apple quarters in a lidded container and cook on high for 6 [4] minutes, until very soft. Stir apple to an even pulp and leave to cool. Stir all remaining ingredients into the cooled apple pulp and mix well. Fill clean jars and seal until ready to use.

NB: Any favourite mincemeat recipes that require cooked apple can be used. The timing for 675 g/1½ lbs apples is 7-8 [6] minutes on high. Because there is no risk of burning apple when cooking in the microwave you do not need to slice them for cooking to a pulp.

Microtip

For cooking cakes do not flour greased baking dishes as this produces an unpleasant coating. Grease and sprinkle with sugar or use a circle of kitchen paper to line the base of the dish (this will peel away easily after cooking).

Timings given are for 650 [750-800] watt ovens

Apple and Walnut Chutney

Cooking Time 15-16 [11] Minutes

Makes approximately 900 g/2 lbs

450 g	*cooking apples, cored and chopped*	*1 lb*
100 g	*carrots, chopped*	*4 oz*
100 g	*dates, chopped*	*4 oz*
50 g	*walnuts, chopped*	*2 oz*
50 g	*raisins*	*2 oz*
3 tbsp	*lemon juice*	*3 tbsp*
225 g	*dark brown sugar*	*8 oz*
1 tsp	*salt*	*1 tsp*
6 tbsp	*cider vinegar*	*6 tbsp*
1 tbsp	*tomato puree*	*1 tbsp*

Combine all ingredients in a large bowl and cook uncovered on high for 15-16 [11] minutes stirring 2 or 3 times, until mixture begins to thicken. Pour into sterilised jars and cover.

Keep several weeks to mature.

Easy

Christmas Punch

Cooking Time 10 [7] Minutes Makes 12 glasses

750 ml	*Dubonnet*	*1¼ pints*
400 ml	*unsweetened pineapple juice*	*14 fl oz*
2 tbsp	*lemon juice*	*2 tbsp*
2 tbsp	*rum*	*2 tbsp*
1	*lemon, sliced*	*1*

Pour the Dubonnet, pineapple and lemon juice into a large bowl. Add 300 ml/½ pint water and heat on high for 10 [6-7] minutes. Add the rum and lemon slices and serve warm.

Spicy Fruit Punch

Cooking Time 14[10] Minutes Makes 25 glasses

2	*lemons*	*2*
1	*orange*	*1*
100 g	*granulated sugar*	*4 oz*
1 litre	*orange juice*	*1¾ pints*
450 ml	*unsweetened pineapple juice*	*¾ pint*
½ tsp	*ground nutmeg*	*½ tsp*
½ tsp	*mixed spice*	*½ tsp*
6	*cloves*	*6*
1 litre	*ginger ale*	*1¾ pints*

Pare the rind from one lemon, squeeze and strain the juice. Slice the second lemon and the orange. Discard any pips. Dissolve the sugar in 600 ml/1 pint of water on high for 4 [3] minutes. Add the orange and pineapple juices, lemon rind and juice, and the spices. Heat on high for a further 6 [4] minutes, then pour in the ginger ale, and reheat on high for 4 [3] minutes. Remove the cloves and lemon rind, and garnish with orange and lemon slices.

Microtip

Citrus fruits will yield more juice if they are heated in the microwave on high for 20-30 seconds before squeezing.

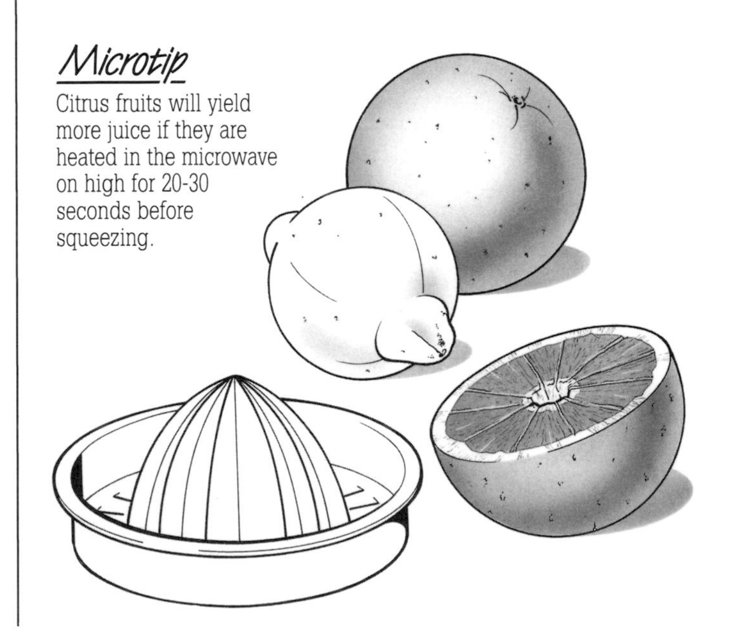

Timings given are for 650 [750-800] watt ovens

Easy

Mulled Wine

Cooking Time 5 [4] Minutes Makes about 6 glasses

600 ml	*red wine*	*1 pint*
6 tbsp	*brandy*	*6 tbsp*
50 g	*sugar*	*2 oz*
1	*cinnamon stick*	*1*
3	*cloves*	*3*
1	*orange, sliced*	*1*
1	*lemon, sliced*	*1*

Combine all the ingredients in a large serving bowl and warm through on high for 5 [4] minutes. Stir well, then pour into glasses.

Easy

Hot Honey and Lemon

Cooking Time 2 [1] Minutes

Makes approximately 250 ml/8 fl oz

2 tbsp	*honey*	*2 tbsp*
	juice of ½ lemon or	
1½ tbsp	*lemon juice*	*1½ tbsp*
250 ml	*water*	*8 fl oz*

Combine the honey and lemon juice in a glass or mug and add water to required amount. Heat on high for 2 [1½] minutes, stir well. Drink while hot.

Easy

Chocolate Fudge

Cooking Time 3 [2] Minutes

100 g	*plain chocolate*	*4 oz*
100 g	*unsalted butter*	*4 oz*
450 g	*icing sugar*	*1 lb*
3 tbsp	*milk*	*3 tbsp*
50 g	*toasted hazlenuts*	*2 oz*

Combine chocolate, butter, icing sugar and milk in a large bowl, cover and cook on high for 3 [2] minutes until melted. Beat until smooth and then stir in the nuts. Turn into a lightly oiled 7" square container and smooth surface. Chill to set then cut into squares.

Rum Truffles

Cooking Time 2 [1] Minutes Approx

100 g	*plain chocolate*	*4 oz*
2 tsp	*rum*	*2 tsp*
1	*egg yolk*	*1*
25 g	*cake crumbs*	*1 oz*
25 g	*icing sugar*	*1 oz*
	chocolate vermicelli	

Melt the chocolate and rum for 1½-2 [1] minutes on high. Stir until well blended. Stir in the egg yolk and place back in the oven for a further 10 seconds. Stir well until the mixture thickens very slightly. Add the cake crumbs and icing sugar and continue stirring until the mixture cools a little. Place the mixture in the fridge and leave until almost set, about 30 minutes.

Divide the mixture into 10-12 pieces, then roll each piece into a small ball. Roll each ball in vermicelli and place in individual cases. Store covered in the refrigerator. Take out of refrigerator 30 minutes before serving.

Timings given are for 650 [750-800] watt ovens

INDEX

Timings given are for 650 [750-800] watt ovens